Sri Lankan Wildlife

A VISITOR'S GUIDE

Gehan de Silva Wijeyeratne

edition

I

www.bradtguides.com

Bradt Travel Guides Ltd, UK
The Globe Pequot Press Inc, USA

First published July 2007

Bradt Travel Guides Ltd
23 High Street, Chalfont St Peter, Bucks SL9 9QE, England
www.bradtguides.com
Published in the USA by The Globe Pequot Press Inc,
246 Goose Lane, PO Box 480, Guilford, Connecticut 06437-0480

British Library Cataloguing in Publication Data
A catalogue record for this book is available from the British Library

ISBN-10: 1 84162 174 9
ISBN-13: 978 1 84162 174 6

Photographs
Palitha Antony (PA), Suresh P Benjamin (SB), Reinhard Dirscherl (RD),
Uditha Hettige (UH), Dharshana Jaywardena (DJ), Roshan Kumara (RK),
Duncan Murrell (DM), K A I Nekaris (KN), Andy Skillen (AS),
Studio Times Ltd (various photographers), WaterFrame (various photographers),
Gehan de Silva de Wijeyeratne (GSW), Wildlife Heritage Trust (WHT)
Front cover Leopard (GSW)
Back cover Serendib scops owl (UH)
Title page Cloudforest at Horton Plains, Asian elephant,
black-lipped lizard (all GSW)

Map Steve Munns

Designed and formatted by Pepenbury Ltd
Printed and bound in India at Ajanta Offset & Packagings Ltd, New Delhi

£3.99
12/12

CONTENTS

Introduction   2
Sri Lanka: a biodiversity jewel 2, How to use this book 5,
The Sri Lankan environment 6

Habitats and Reserves   9
Habitats 10, National parks and reserves 16

Mammals   21
Asian elephant 22, Ungulates 26, Carnivores 31,
Primates 40, Squirrels 45, Bats 47, Other mammals 49

Birds   51
Birds of town and garden 52, Birds of the rainforest 55,
Birds of the highlands 58, Birds of the dry lowlands 59,
Birds of the wetlands 62, Birds of the coast 66,
Endemic birds 68

Reptiles and Amphibians   75
Lizards 76, Snakes 82, Crocodiles 88,
Turtles, terrapins and tortoises 91, Amphibians 94

Invertebrates   97
Lower invertebrates 98, Arthropods 99, Butterflies 105,
Dragonflies and damselflies 108

The Underwater World   111
Freshwater fish 112, Marine life 114, Under the sea 115,
Marine mammals 119

Getting About   125
Independent travel 126, Tours 127, Suggested itinerary 128,
Photography tips 130

Further Information   132
Books 132, Societies 134, Finding out more 135

Index   136

Features
    Where to watch primates in Sri Lanka   44
    Watching nocturnal wildlife   50
    Snake bites   87
    Nesting sea turtles in Sri Lanka   93

AUTHOR AND PRINCIPAL PHOTOGRAPHER

Gehan de Silva Wijeyeratne is an internationally published writer and photographer. His books, more than ten, include *Magic of Sri Lanka*, *Portrait of Sri Lanka* and *Leopards and other Wildlife of Yala*. He is a columnist on the monthly business magazine, *LMD*, and the bi-monthly lifestyle magazine, *Living*, and frequently appears on television.

Gehan graduated in civil engineering from Imperial College, London, and qualified as a chartered accountant with Deloittes Touche Tohmatsu in London. After 11 years in the British financial sector, working for LIFFE, Abbey National and Sumitomo Finance, he returned to Sri Lanka. A dual national (British and Sri Lankan) he is presently CEO of the Jetwing Eco Holidays subsidiary and the director for ecotourism of the hotel arm of one of Sri Lanka's leading leisure groups.

ACKNOWLEDGEMENTS

Many people have assisted me over the years in my quest to discover my homeland, Sri Lanka. My colleagues at Jetwing support my efforts to develop Sri Lanka as a destination for nature tourism. Hiran Cooray in particular has shared my vision of tourism's potential as a strong force for conservation. A very special thanks to the office team past and present at Eco Holidays (*www.jetwingeco.com*): Chandrika Maelge, Ajanthan Shanthiratnam, Ayanthi Samarajewa, Renuka Batagoda, Aruni Hewage, Shehani Seneviratne and L de S Gunasekera. Their efficiency has made it possible for me to write about and photograph the beauty of this island. The field staff of the Department of Wildlife Conservation and of the Forest Department, naturalist guides, safari jeep drivers and many others have patiently accompanied me in the field and shared their knowledge and experience. Many Jetwing Eco Holidays naturalist guides have also made it easier for me to find and photograph plants and animals. A special mention goes to Wicky Wickremesekera, and to my friend Lester Perera who has helped many times.

For certain sections, I have modified articles of mine already published elsewhere. My thanks go to the editors of these publications for allowing me to do so. They include Lyn Hughes, managing editor of *Wanderlust*, Krishan Senaratne, former managing editor of *Serendipity*, David Cromack, former editor of *Bird Watching* magazine, and Steve Peaple, editor of *Serendib*. The introductory essay on wildlife is heavily based on a piece for *Discover Sri Lanka*, a publication of the Sri Lanka Tourist Board, and is used with changes with their permission. The mammals chapter has borrowed heavily from a pocket photographic guide published by Jetwing Eco Holidays. I would also like to thank my editor, Mike Unwin, for all his work on the manuscript and the many significant contributions he has made to the text. Thanks also to Anna Moores, Tricia Hayne, Caroline Mardall and Hilary Bradt for their support and work on the book.

My mother, my Aunt Vijita and my sister Manouri started me off on photography. My wife Nirma and my daughters Maya and Amali are patient and give me space, even when I spend my family holidays working on the 'next book'.

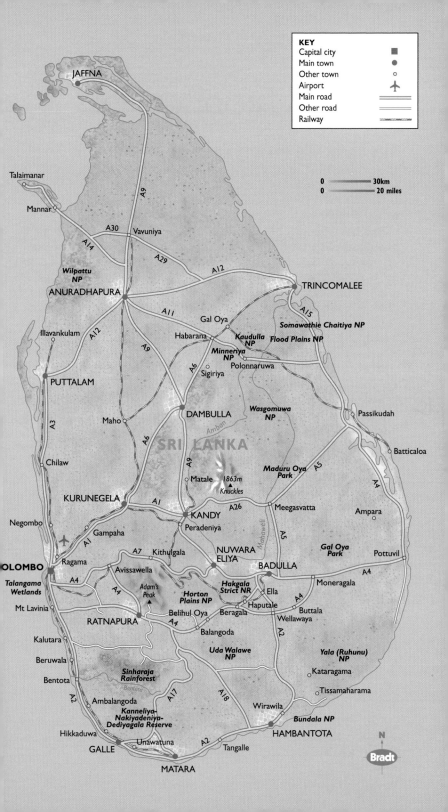

INTRODUCTION

SRI LANKA: A BIODIVERSITY JEWEL

How many destinations in the world allow a visitor to snorkel by day off golden-sand beaches and then search by nightfall for leopards? Sri Lanka must surely be one of the very few, with a breathtaking array of landscapes and wildlife packed into its relatively small area.

At around 66,000km², Sri Lanka is only about half the size of England. Yet this small island confounds the usual norms of biogeography by being home to a wealth of large mammals. It is, for instance, the best place in Asia to see the continent's largest terrestrial mammal, the Asian elephant, with up to 300 gathering annually around the receding shores of the Minneriya National Park. It also offers that ultimate ecotourism trump card, the leopard. In fact Yala National Park has one of the highest densities of this elusive animal anywhere in the world, with the combination of the open terrain and the cat's confidence as top island predator making for some fine leopard viewing.

The island also has among the world's highest species density for other faunal groups, including reptiles, birds and amphibians. Tree frogs, for instance, are most associated with Costa Rica, yet ongoing research suggests that Sri Lanka may yet emerge as the frog capital of the world. This is due to a prolific species radiation, whereby the diversity of available ecological niches has allowed certain species to evolve into many others. The cloudforests that cloak the island's mountainous core harbour other unique animals, such as the dwarf lizard, which has a prehensile tail and gives birth to live young. Still more species doubtless await discovery in the richly biodiverse rainforests of the island's southwest.

The attractions of Sri Lanka's biodiversity and compact size are supported by its good tourist infrastructure, with excellent hotels, extensive roads, and widely spoken English. Many top cultural sites are also good for ecotourists, with archaeological reserves doubling up as nature reserves – take the medieval capital of Polonnaruwa, among whose ancient stupas and sublime stone sculptures, birders can see more than a hundred species in a day. This combination of culture, nature and friendly people justifies Sri Lanka's fast-growing reputation as one of Asia's very best ecotourism destinations.

Sadly Sri Lanka has all too often hit the headlines for the wrong reasons – principally the protracted armed struggle between the Liberation Tigers of Tamil Eelam ('Tamil Tigers') and the government. Today, however, both parties continue to re-affirm their commitment to a ceasefire signed in 2003. Sporadic fighting continues in a few places, but the problem areas lie mainly in the north and east and have never been on wildlife itineraries. Even when a situation of open conflict existed, wildlife enthusiasts continued to travel safely to the rich wildlife areas in the south-west, which lie far from the troubles. It is hoped that mounting international pressure will force both parties to broker a permanent peace.

The Toque monkey is one of two endemic primates that is active during the day. (GSW)

The Boxing Day tsunami of 2004 also took a heavy toll on Sri Lanka, leaving 35,000 dead. However, the environmental damage was largely limited to a narrow coastal strip extending no more than 100m inland, except at lagoons and estuaries. The coastal environment bounced back very quickly and within a couple of years there were few physical signs left of the devastation. Sadly, many families will continue to endure the emotional trauma of lost lives and livelihoods. By visiting Sri Lanka as a responsible ecotourist, you will be helping to support and rebuild these communities.

Shaheen falcon (GSW)

HOW TO USE THIS BOOK

Sri Lanka has a bewildering variety of wildlife and a book of this size cannot hope to do justice to it all. Instead, it offers a balanced and colourful overview of the island's wildlife from a visitor's perspective, while giving some insight into its natural environment. Those with a more specific interest, for example in birds, will need the relevant field guides (see *Further information*) to find out more.

Major taxonomic groups that visitors are likely to notice each described here in a separate chapter. The text does not focus on identification – that's what field guides are for – but aims to introduce the animals, and to describe the most interesting aspects of their behaviour and ecology. The selection of species reflects those that are most interesting or most typical of the island, and also those that the average visitor is most likely to encounter. In the case of insects, for instance, it would be impossible in a book of this size to tackle the vast array of beetles, weevils, crickets and others that make up this huge class. I have, instead, focused on the fascinating, beautiful and highly visible butterflies and dragonflies.

Coral tree (*Erithryna variegata*) in flower (GSW)

Taxonomic order is treated flexibly, and in some cases is bypassed for easier reference (birds, for instance, are considered primarily by habitat). Nonetheless, a basic grasp of taxonomic terminology is helpful – as in the two following simplified examples:

	Leopard	**Bue-tailed bee-eater**
Kingdom	Animalia (animals)	Animalia (animals)
Phylum	Chordata (vertebrates)	Chordata (vertebrates)
Class	Mammalia (mammals)	Aves (birds)
Order	Carnivora (carnivores)	Coraciiformes (near-passerines)
Family	Felidae (cats)	Meropidae (bee-eaters)
Genus	*Panthera* (big cats)	*Merops* (typical bee-eaters)
Species	*Panthera pardus* (leopard)	*Merops philippinus* (blue-tailed bee-eater)

This chapter gives some background to the Sri Lankan environment, with an overview of its climate and geology. Chapter two, *Habitats and Reserves*, describes and locates the island's major habitat types, and also the best places for watching wildlife. Chapter seven, *Getting About*, offers advice on how to make the most of your trip, while *Further information* directs you to useful background reading and key contact details.

Other chapters are arranged broadly around the major groups into which animals are classified, with specific examples chosen from each that reflect the interests of most visitors. These groups are mammals, birds, reptiles, amphibians and invertebrates. Finally, there is a section on underwater life, including Sri Lanka's rich marine environment, which seldom gets the attention it deserves.

THE SRI LANKAN ENVIRONMENT
WEATHER AND CLIMATE

Sri Lanka can be broadly divided by the interaction of rainfall and topography into three climatic zones, namely the low country wet zone, the hill zone and the low country dry zone. The country's topography comprises coastal lowlands that spread inland and ascend sharply to mountains, rising to over 2,400m in the southern half. In fact the island can be divided into three peneplains (horizontal layers formed by erosion). The lowest of these is from 0–30m, the second rises to 480m and the third to 1,800m. Rainfall is heavily influenced by the central hills, and falls during two seasons: the southwest monsoon (May–August) and northeast monsoon (October–January).

The low country wet zone

The humid, lowland wet zone in the southwest of the island has no marked seasons, being fed by both the southwest monsoon and the northeast monsoon. It receives 2,000–5,000mm of rain from the southwest monsoon and afternoon showers from the northeast monsoon. Humidity is high, rarely dropping below 97%, while temperatures range from 27°–31°C over the year.

The low country wet zone is the most densely populated area in Sri Lanka. The coast is well settled, while the interior has coconut and rubber plantations, some rice cultivation and small industries. Remnants of rainforest and tropical moist forest exist tenuously in some parts of the interior, under pressure from an expanding population. It is in these forests that many of Sri Lanka's sought-after endemic species are found.

The hill zone

The mountainous interior lies within the wet zone and rises to over 2,400m. It is intensively planted with tea, but also has small areas of remnant forest and open grassland. Rainfall is generally well distributed, except in the Uva Province which gets very little from June to September.

Temperatures are cooler than in the lowlands: in the mid elevations, such as the area around Kandy, they vary from 17°C to 31°C throughout the year; in the cooler mountains, they vary from 14°C to 32°C. Mornings can be chilly, and December and January may bring frost in the higher hills, when night-time temperatures fall to below zero.

Low country dry zone

The rest of the country, more than two-thirds of Sri Lanka's land area, consists of the dry zone of the northern, southern and eastern plains. These regions receive 600–1,900mm of rain each year, mainly from the northeast monsoon. The dry zone is further divided into the arid zones of the northwest and southeast, which receive less than 600mm of rain, as these areas are not in the direct path of the monsoonal rains.

The coastal plains in the Southern Province and North Central Province are dry and hot. Much of this zone is under rice and other field crops, irrigated by vast man-

Horton Plains National Park protects a mix of grassland, cloud forest and steep escarpments. (GSW)

made lakes (the 'tanks'), many of which are centuries old and were built by royal decree to capture the scarce rainfall. Once the 'granary of the east', exporting rice as far as China and Burma, the dry zone was devastated by a combination of war and disease. The once bountiful rice plains were reclaimed by scrub jungle, the haunt of elephant, bear and leopard. Since independence in 1948, successive governments have vigorously promoted resettlement of these areas. Sandy beaches fringe the coastline and it is always possible to find one that is away from the path of the prevailing monsoon.

WHEN TO TRAVEL

Sri Lanka's pronounced climatic variation means that different regions appeal most at different times of the year, and there is usually some part of the country that is dry and enjoying good weather. The inter-monsoonal lull falls between February and April. February is the driest in the areas generally visited by those interested in culture and natural history. The period from January to April is the warmest in the lowlands, but is the favoured time for many tourists as it is generally the driest and also coincides with the Northern winter. The highlands may experience frost during January and February. The best time for birdwatchers extends from November to April when there is less rainfall, with migrants at this time boosting the tally of birds. Wildlife viewing in the dry zone national parks is good during the hot, dusty summer months between May and August, when streams are reduced to a mere trickle and animals concentrate around waterholes. The west and southern coastal seas are calmest from November to April, with the first three months of the year providing the best visibility for diving and snorkelling.

GEOLOGY

Sri Lanka's diverse geology has long attracted commercial interests, and from ancient times the island has been famous for its gemstone deposits.

In prehistoric times what is now Sri Lanka was a part of the ancient landmass of Gondwanaland. Towards the end of the Mesozoic era this began breaking up into the crustal plates that held Africa, India and Australasia. Sri Lanka was a part of the Indian plate that 45 million years ago collided with the Asian plate, creating the Himalayas. Some 20 million years ago during the Miocene, shallow seas covered the lowlands of Sri Lanka. The limestone beds in this area today exhibit characteristic limestone formations such as grikes, caverns and sinkholes.

In the lowlands, the estuaries and floodplains have large deposits of alluvium from the heavy soil load carried down by monsoonal floods. Sand dunes are common along the south and east coasts, with their orientation influenced by the direction of the monsoon winds. The continental shelf around the island varies in extent from 8km to 40km. At the edge of the shelf is a steep slope dissected by submarine valleys that come within a few kilometres of the coastline.

The underlying geology of the island is largely composed of ancient crystalline rocks of Precambrian origin. Three complexes are recognised within these rocks. The largest is the highland series that runs from southwest to northeast, encompassing much of the hill country. To the west and east of this respectively are the western and eastern Vijayan complexes. The highland series consists predominantly of metamorphosed sediments, and has a long parallel series of folds termed the Taprobanian fold system. The Vijayan complex is a varied group of gneisses and granites and does not show any regular folding. In the southwest, the southwestern group has a rock structure similar to the highland group, with metasediments and charnockitic gneisses together with migmatitic and granitic gneisses. In this region there is also a distinctive band of rocks about 5km wide and 80km long, termed the Sinharaja basic zone.

A key feature of the island's topography is its three peneplains. One of the best places to appreciate these is Ella Gap, renowned also for its scenic views. The lowest

Eroded rock formations at Ussangoda
(Nihal Fernando/Studio Times)

peneplain is flat, with the exception of a few rocky outcrops, such as Sigiriya, many of which support archaeological or religious structures. The middle peneplain rises to about 480m. On the highest peneplain is the famous Horton Plains National Park, which has a number of rugged mountain peaks.

In the 1980s engineers constructing a dam in Maduru Oya were surprised to uncover an ancient dam. This suggested that engineers from the past, in constructing large earthworks, had an appreciation of the fundamentals of geology. However, there is much still to be learnt today.

HABITATS
AND RESERVES

Morning mist, Horton Plains (CSW)

Lowland rainforest at Sinharaja (Studio Times)

HABITATS

LOWLAND RAINFOREST

The lowland rainforests of Sri Lanka occur in the southwest of the island in the low country wet zone. They are found at largely below 1,000m in elevation, where the warm, wet conditions and evenly distributed rainfall provide the climate for a luxuriant growth of plants. Physical factors, such as soil, slope and rainfall, are key in determining which plants become the climax species, ie: those that predominate when the rainforest is left undisturbed. The tallest trees average a height of 30m or more. Most belong to the family Dipterocarpaceae, an Asian group extending from India to China and Indonesia. Around 50 species of this family are found in Sri Lanka, all but one endemic. The growth of Dipterocarps requires fungi called ecto-mycorrhiza – though these are not specific to individual species, unlike the more famous association between mycorrhiza and orchids. Rainforest trees often engage in mass flowering and fruiting, which may trigger seasonal movements of birds from higher elevations to take advantage of this rich food source.

Contrary to popular belief, rainforests are often found on poor soil. This is why the soil becomes totally impoverished after just one or two harvests when they are cleared for agriculture. Roots of rainforest trees are often shallow and run along the surface where the nutrients are concentrated. Almost all of the organic mass of the rainforest is above the ground. In fact, nutrients shed in the form of fallen leaves and dead animals are rapidly recycled by a vast array of organisms, from microbial bacteria and fungi to earthworms and other invertebrates.

Many rainforest trees have buttress roots for support on the thin soils. Unusually, the Dipterocarps do not, and their large, straight trunks are prone to toppling. This creates open spaces with abundant light, allowing new trees to take their place. Saplings can lie in a dormant state of growth for many years. Those that look less

10

than a year old may actually be several decades old. Unless a tree fall creates the right conditions of light and humidity, the saplings can't easily reach the light at the top of the canopy. Water is also a key factor in determining the growth and species density of rainforest plants, with wetter areas having a higher diversity of species. Amongst the Dipterocarps, for example, the genus *Vatica* occurs in the dry zone in gallery forests, but only along riverbanks.

Sri Lanka's rainforests are vital for conserving its biodiversity. Some 24% of Sri Lankan plants, comprising more than 830 species in 25 genera, are endemic to the island. Of these, 60% are found in the rainforest and 40% are confined to it. The Sri Lankan rainforest provides a link between the rainforests of Africa and southeast Asia, because of its origins in the ancient continent of Gondwanaland. Thus it has an ancient floral affinity with the African continent. The subsequent link with the Asian mainland allowed mainland species to colonise the island during periods when a land bridge was present and climatic conditions were suitable. As climates changed, species were left marooned on the island, resulting in relict species and causing new species to evolve.

Sadly, only an estimated 2% of Sri Lanka has rainforests left, a tiny fraction of what there was just a few centuries ago. Much of what remains, estimated in total at a mere 750km², consists of heavily disturbed fragments. The largest stretch is the Kanneliya-Nakiyadeniya-Dediyagala forest reserve complex in the Galle district (see page 44), but this has been badly affected by human intervention and is poor in its animal life. The Sinharaja Man and Biosphere Reserve (see page 18) is smaller, but represents the largest single undisturbed rainforest remnant.

Sri Lanka's rainforests are also of vital importance to people. They conserve the hydrological cycle on which agriculture is dependent: without rainforests, the rivers would literally run dry and temperatures would rise. They are also an important carbon sink, and a genetic reservoir of plants and animals whose genes may be commercially valuable for medicines and other products. Increasingly the rainforests are becoming important as a recreational resource, too.

Top Pitcher plants (Nepenthaceae) are carnivorous rainforest plants. (Studio Times.)
Above Rainforests help control the water cycle. (UH).

CLOUDFOREST

The cloudforests are the naturally occurring forests of the hills. They hold a relict fauna that hails from the age when Sri Lanka was part of the ancient supercontinent of Gondwanaland, contiguous with present-day Antarctica. The flora of Sri Lanka's cloudforests is thus a key to the past, to the age of dinosaurs.

Typically cloudforests, or upper montane forests, start to grow at around 1,500m, although sub-montane cloudforests on the eastern slopes of Sinharaja can occur at only 800m. Generally about 2,000mm of annual rainfall is needed for wet, evergreen rainforests to grow in the tropics: if the rainfall is less, or too irregular, deciduous forests or dry evergreen forests occur instead. At high elevations, however, the upward movement of cool air that condenses into mist provides horizontal precipitation, which means that rainfall as low as 1,500mm will still produce wet evergreen forests.

In lowland rainforest the dominant trees are giants that exceed 30m. Cloudforest trees, by contrast, are stunted, standing mostly 3–4m in height and seldom exceeding 10m. They are gnarled in appearance, with umbrella-shaped crowns and leathery leaves to resist the wind and sun. Despite the extreme climate at high elevations, their limbs are densely covered with mosses, lichens and ferns. These absorb plentiful moisture from clouds of mist that drift through the forest, in a process known as 'fog-stripping'. Some scientists believe that they absorb more moisture from this source than they do from rain.

Cloudforests play an important role in conserving water. They absorb rainfall like a sponge and release it gradually into the many streams that criss-cross the highlands.

Cloudforest at Horton Plains National Park (Studio Times)

This helps prevent destructive flash floods by ensuring a steady source of water trickling into streams during dry weather. Where the cloudforests have been extensively cleared, there are flash floods and soil erosion during the rains and severe droughts in dry weather.

Half of the trees found in Sri Lanka's cloudforests are endemic to the island, with another 40% being endemic to Sri Lanka and southern India. The cloudforests also support a rich epiphytic flora, including many species of orchid. In the undergrowth are several plants of the genus *Strobilanthes*, some of which have a flowering cycle spaced as many as seven years apart. When a mass flowering occurs, birds and animals from the lower slopes flock to the feast. Among various animals confined to Sri Lanka's cloudforests are several lizards (see page 77), and birds such as the Ceylon whistling-thrush (see page 72).

As a result of its long isolation from nearby mountain ranges, Sri Lanka has no native conifers. Strangely a few species of plants in the genera *Rhododenron*, *Prunus*, *Ilex*, *Vaccinium* and *Euonymus* have found their way to the mountains of Sri Lanka and south India. There is no satisfactory explanation

The black-lipped lizard (*top*, GSW) and Ceylon whistling thrush (*above*, GSW) are both species that are restricted to Sri Lanka's highlands.

for how these montane plants managed to spread across large distances between mountain ranges. Many of Sri Lanka's montane plants are derived from lowland species adapting through evolution to the cooler highlands. The genera *Syzygium* and *Eugenia* are two examples, between them contributing more than 20 species to the cloudforests.

Cloudforests are slow to regenerate. The low temperatures at high elevations retard growth, unlike the prolific growth in the wet, warm lowlands. This has led to the use of introduced conifers to afforest denuded hillsides, which consequently tend to be devoid of local fauna and flora. Fortunately more than half of Sri Lanka's native high-elevation forests have been spared, although much of the lower montane forest has been cleared for coffee and subsequently tea. Nevertheless, as a proportion of the land area of Sri Lanka, these forests occupy less than 1%. The best place to see cloudforest is at Horton Plains National Park (see page 19). Other examples are found at the Hakgala Botanical Gardens near Nuwara Eliya, Corbett's Gap at the Knuckles, which is also good for wildlife, and at the Peak Wilderness Sanctuary, which can be viewed from the trails near Adam's Peak.

The dry lowlands of Wasgomuwa National Park lie to the north of the Knuckles massif. (GSW)

DRY LOWLAND FOREST

Dry lowland forests occur in the dry lowland zone, which covers more than two-thirds of Sri Lanka. They encompass a variety of vegetation types, including deciduous monsoon forest, riparian (or riverside) forest, thorn scrub, sand dune habitats and mangroves.

The exact species dominant in any area will depend on factors such as soil and rainfall, but broad generalisations can be made. In the southern dry zone, in Yala for example, evergreen species such as palu (*Manilkara hexandra*) and weera (*Drypetes sepiara*) dominate. The palu attains a height of 20m in these conditions. Taller species include the woodapple tree (*Limonia acidissima*), mee (*Madhuca longifolia*), ehela (*Cassia fistula*) and kunumella (*Diospyros ovalifolia*). The fruit of the woodapple is popular with elephants, which help to propagate it by dispersing the seeds in their droppings.

Dry evergreen forests usually have a broken canopy, allowing a plentiful shrub layer to flourish below. Some shrubs live in partial shade while others thrive in open areas. One that seems to thrive in the open is the ranawara (*Cassia auriculata*). Other small trees and shrubs include andara (*Dichrostachys cinerea*), karamba (*Carissa spinarum*), agil (*Erythroxylum monogynum*) and maila (*Bahunia racemosa*). In more saline areas close to the coast, one of the dominant shrubs is the maliththan (*Salvadora persica*).

Moist deciduous forests are found in the dry lowlands, where the moisture content is higher due to factors such as heavier rainfall, more retention of soil water or a higher water table. These deciduous forests are medium to high in stature, with a canopy of around 20m in height. They support species such as burutha (*Chloroxylon swietenia*), milla (*Vitex altissima*), kon (*Schleicheria oleosa*) and velang (*Pterospermum*

14

suberifolium). The canopy also includes evergreen species such as palu, weera and kohomba (*Azadirachta indica*), while the shrubs include kukurumana (*Catunaregam spinosa*) and korakoha (*Memecylon umbellatum*).

Tropical thorn forests are lower in stature and scrubbier in appearance. Many shrub species found in the dry evergreen forests are also found here, including ranawara, andara and maliththan. Other species include katupila (*Maytenus emarginata*), dodampana (*Glycosmis mauritiana*) and kukrumana.

Grasslands, too, are a feature of the dry lowlands. These may be open or shaded, and some are subject to seasonal flooding – a good example being on the bed of the Minneriya Lake, which is the setting for 'The Gathering' of elephants. Many grassland plants are short-lived and exploit the rainy season. Open grasslands are dominated by *Chloris barabata* and species in the genus *Eragrostis*. The carnivorous plant watessa (*Drosera burmannii*) is also found at disturbed sites. Shaded grasslands have species such as buffalo grass (*Stenotaphrum dimidiatum*). The alien Pethi thora (*Cassia thora*) and lantana (*Lantana camara*) have invaded open areas in some national parks, and are being removed to allow the grasslands to regenerate. In seasonally flooded grasslands, the thorny herb neeramulliya (*Hygrophila schulli*), and grasses such as welmaruk (*Echinochloa crusgalli*) and etavara (*Panicum repens*) are found.

Riparian gallery forests in the dry zone are dominated by tall kumbuk trees (*Terminalia arjuna*) that line the riverbanks. Other water-loving trees include Indian willow (*Polyalthia longifolia*), and moist forest species such as halmilla (*Berrya cordifolia*) and damba (*Syzygium gardneri*). Many riparian forest trees also occur in moist deciduous forest.

Mangroves are found in brackish water along the coastline. Sri Lanka has 23 species recognised as true mangrove plants, together with other plants that are known as mangrove associates. Common mangrove species include kadol (*Rhizophora mucronata*), manda (*Avicennia marina*), thelakiriya (*Excoecaria agallocha*), katuikili (*Acanthus ilicifolius*) and beriya (*Lumnitzera racemosa*). The kirala tree (*Sonneratia caseolaris*) is a tall mangrove plant that forms dense stands. The fruit is used for making fruit juice and ice cream.

Top Elephants gather on the open grasslands of Minneriya National Park. (Studio Times)
Above Mangroves are threatened by coastal development. (Studio Times).

'Elephant Rock' seen from across the scenic Buttuwa Wewa in Yala National Park. (GSW)

NATIONAL PARKS AND RESERVES

Sri Lanka has 21 national parks, which fall under the jurisdiction of the Department of Wildlife Conservation (DWLC). A number of other forest reserves and sanctuaries fall under the jurisdiction of the Forest Department (FD). A few wetland sites and archaeological sites are also important nature reserves. Some of the key sites are described below.

YALA (RUHUNU) NATIONAL PARK

Ruhunu National Park is located in the southeast corner of the island in the lowland dry zone. Most people refer to this park as Yala National Park, or simply Yala, although Ruhunu National Park is its officially gazetted name. The original block of land that was designated as a game sanctuary and subsequently a national park is known as Block 1. Four other blocks have since been acquired for the national park. Visitors are restricted to Block 1, with visits to Blocks 2–5 requiring special permission. However, since game viewing is best in Block 1, there is little need for casual visitors to see the others. The park is adjoined to the east by Yala East National Park, though the condition of the roads does not make visits to this area practicable at present. Together, the two national parks and their adjoining smaller reserves and sanctuaries make up a total area of just over 1,500km² – approximately 2.5% of Sri Lanka's land area.

Yala is the premier national park of Sri Lanka and arguably one of the best in Asia for mammals. The top draw is the Sri Lankan leopard, a subspecies endemic to Sri Lanka, which occurs here in unusually high densities. During the fruiting of the palu trees (the dominant species in the area) in June and July, sloth bears are also often observed. Other animals that visitors have a reasonable chance of seeing include elephant, sambar, spotted deer, buffalo, wild pig, both stripe-necked and ruddy mongoose, Hanuman langur, toque macaque (or monkey), golden jackal and Indian palm-civet. The park's picturesque landscapes include a large stretch of coastline and impressive rock outcrops. The combination of freshwater and marine habitats, scrub and pockets of dense woodland makes for a high diversity of bird species: over 220 have been recorded, with serious birdwatchers notching up to 100 in a single day during migration. Serious birdwatchers should also consider visits to Bundala National Park (an hour away) or the Palatupana Salt Pans (ten minutes away), especially for migrant shorebirds.

UDA WALAWE NATIONAL PARK

This park, just over 300km² in extent, lies south of the central mountains in the southern half of the island. Created to protect the watershed of the enormous Uda Walawe reservoir, it has extensive stretches of grassland as well as scrub jungle and riverine forest. The park is the best place in the whole of Asia for observing wild Asian elephants; sightings are virtually guaranteed, even with just a single game drive. It is less good for viewing other mammals, though in recent years jungle cat and even leopard sightings have been reported regularly. Birdwatchers will enjoy the presence of raptors such as crested hawk eagle, serpent eagle, white-bellied sea eagle, grey-headed fish eagle and others.

Uda Walawe National Park at dawn
(Nihal Fernando/Studio Times)

Grey-headed fish eagle (GSW)

WASGOMUWA NATIONAL PARK

Wasgomuwa, just under 400km² in extent, is situated in the dry lowlands of the North Central Province, north of the highly biodiverse Knuckles Massif. All the big game is found here, including possibly the highest density of sloth bears in the country, although both this and leopard are elusive. The park is an excellent location for observing family units of elephants, which are still relatively wild and unpredictable. At present there is little visitor traffic, but this may change if access from Polonnaruwa improves.

The rainforest canopy towers 30m at Sinharaja. (UH)

SINHARAJA RAINFOREST

Situated in the wet southwest of the island, this reserve of 112km² is managed by the Forest Department and is Sri Lanka's premier rainforest. More than half the trees here are found nowhere else in the world. Sinharaja's feeding parties of birds are the subject of one of the longest-running ornithological studies in the world, and are the highlight of any birding visit. Different species work collectively like a giant vacuum cleaner, devouring prey in its path. Except for a few montane species, almost all of the Sri Lankan endemic birds can be seen here, including the Ceylon rufous babbler, whose constant medley of squeaks and chatters betrays the presence of a feeding party, and the furtive and easily overlooked red-faced malkoha.

MINNERIYA AND KAUDULLA NATIONAL PARKS

These two parks are each sited around a large reservoir, and lie within half an hour's drive of one another in the North Central Province. Many mammals frequent the scrub jungle around the lakes, but they are generally hard to see – except for elephants. During September and October an annual concentration of elephants, known as 'The Gathering', assembles on the receding shoreline of the Minneriya Lake in Minneriya National Park. Small family groups arrive from scrub jungles tens of kilometres apart and coalesce into small herds, which in turn congregate into larger herds of 50–100. Visitors have often counted over 300 elephants at one time. It is, by any standards, a spectacular wildlife event.

HORTON PLAINS NATIONAL PARK

In the central highlands, Horton Plains is the highest plateau on the island, with temperatures sometimes falling below zero at night. The cloudforests here, a mere 30km^2 in extent, are rich in endemic plants and animals. Birds such as the Ceylon whistling-thrush and Ceylon bush warbler are best seen here – as is the unique dwarf lizard, found only in the montane zone.

WILPATTU NATIONAL PARK

Wilpattu is situated in the dry lowlands to the northwest of Sri Lanka. It is the island's largest single national park, with an area of 1,316km^2, and protects a series of lakes or 'villus', which have varying degrees of freshness or salinity. The park reopened in 2003 after being closed for nearly 15 years. The Tamil Tigers (LTTE)

Adam's Peak, seen from Horton Plains National Park (GSW)

Pink lotus blossoms are an attractive feature of Sri Lanka's wetland areas. (GSW)

uses parts of the park as a conduit for men and materials. At the time of going to print, the prevailing security situation made visits inadvisable. Over time, the park's wildlife should regain its former abundance and become more habituated to vehicles. Wilpattu was once known for its leopards, and big cat enthusiasts are hoping that, given time, leopard viewing will again come to the fore. Together with Yala, Wilpattu is also the best place to see the sloth bear. Other mammals in Wilpattu are similar to Yala's, though visitors may also see the muntjac or barking deer.

TALANGAMA WETLAND
The Talangama Wetland is a surprising little jewel that ranks among the country's top nature sites, both because of its richness and because of its accessibility from Colombo. At night a host of mammals come out of hiding, including porcupines, fishing cats, ring-tailed civets, common palm civets, brown mongooses, black-naped hares and the endemic spotted mouse-deer. Daytime belongs to the birds (more than a hundred species have been recorded), and the colourful butterflies and dragonflies. The critically endangered western race of the purple-faced leaf monkey booms from the treetops, and the water monitor, a gigantic lizard related to the Komodo dragon, prowls the waterways.

SIGIRIYA SANCTUARY
Sigiriya is one of the most highly rated archaeological sites in Sri Lanka and centres around the Sigiriya rock, an inselberg that juts about 200m above the surrounding dry lowlands. In the 5th century AD, King Kasyappa made it the focus of his palace and at the base of the rock are several hundred acres of landscaped gardens surrounded by a moat. Sigiriya is a mad genius king's vision of a heaven on earth, with frescoes of mysterious bare-breasted maidens who attract scholarly debate. It is also one of the best places in Sri Lanka for watching primates, which find plentiful forest cover in the surrounding dry zone woodland, and water from the moat and ponds. What's more, people do not chase them away. Four of Sri Lanka's five primate species are found here: the hanuman langur, the endemic toque macaque, the endemic purple-faced leaf monkey (the northern race) and at night, the grey loris.

MAMMALS

Asian elephant bathing (AS)

Mammals, of which we human are one species, constitute one of five classes of vertebrates (animals with a backbone), the others being birds, reptiles, amphibians and fish. They are distinguished by a number of general characteristics. These include the presence of fur or hair, giving birth to live young (although the egg-laying echidna and platypus in Australia are exceptions), and the young suckling milk from their mother. Sri Lanka has more just over 90 species of terrestrial mammals and close to 30 species of marine mammals, which range from the five-tonne bull Asian elephant – the second-largest land mammal on earth – to the diminutive pygmy shrew, no larger than a matchbox.

ASIAN ELEPHANT

Sri Lanka is *the* place to see the Asian elephant, with sightings virtually guaranteed in Uda Walawe and regular in a number of other parks. Elephants are seen throughout the year, though are never predictable: at times several families may be seen in the space of a single day; at other times they may disappear for several days at a time. Research undertaken with radio-collared elephants shows that lone bulls are more prone to range outside parks during the dry season. In the absence of detailed records, it is hard to discern a clear pattern. The most spectacular elephant event in Sri Lanka – or indeed anywhere in Asia – is 'The Gathering', which takes place at both Minneriya National Park and Kaudulla in August and September. At its peak, over 300 elephants may gather within just a few square kilometres. The author has also seen herds of over 50 in Minneriya at other times of the year.

The Asian elephant is one of three species that make up the family Elephantidae,

in the order Proboscidea. It is distinguished from the African elephant by its smaller ears and concave back. African elephants – at least those of the better-known savanna species – are also bigger, and both the males and females carry tusks. The Asian elephant is now restricted to 13 countries. The race found in Sri Lanka is larger than that in India and is considered to be a separate subspecies. It does not engage in long migrations.

Each tusker at Yala can be identified by its unique combination of features. Nalaka, pictured here, has become a 'personality' loved by regular visitors to the park. (GSW)

Play among sub-adult elephants is vital for building social bonds. (GSW)

In Sri Lanka, only 7–8% of male elephants carry tusks. It isn't known whether this has always been the case, or whether it results from males with tusks having being removed from the gene pool by hunting. What we do know is that the tusks are actually modified incisor teeth. The surface of each molar tooth has transverse ridges that help the elephant to grind down its food. Elephants can go through six sets of molars in a lifetime, and eventually die of starvation when the last set is worn down. They eat around 150kg of vegetable matter a day. This passes rapidly through their system, as elephants lack the four-chambered stomach of most ruminants. Special bacteria in their gut help break down the cellulose-heavy diet.

On one visit to Yala I observed a baby elephant eating the dung of its adult relatives. This may seem revolting to us, but it is a matter of life or death to a young elephant. A baby isn't born with the gut bacteria it needs to digest food, thus it has to ingest this bacteria from the dung of adults. Elephants deposit about 100kg of dung every day. This relatively digested vegetable matter is important for the maintenance of their ecosystem. Certain species of plants are dispersed as seeds in the dung, while other plants benefit from a pile of organic manure to help them grow.

Almost everything about the elephant is extraordinary and demands superlatives. Its trunk is a specially modified nose that is used as a fifth limb, a weapon and for visual communication. The soles of its feet have special cells called paccinian corpuscles, arranged like layers of an onion with a gelatinous layer in between, which act as seismic phones and allow elephants to 'listen' with their feet. Elephants can communicate by stamping their feet and generating seismic waves over several kilometres. They also use low-frequency sounds inaudible to us, known as infrasounds, by which different clans can communicate over many kilometres. Sometimes the behaviour of an elephant reveals that it is engaged in infrasound conversation with another elephant that is out of sight.

A baby elephant is born into a tight-knit family dominated by females. The simplest unit in elephant society is the mother and calf. A bond group is formed with other female adult elephants, which help to raise the baby and are called 'allo' mothers ('allo' being the technical term for an act perfomed for one animal by another). A baby elephant grows up with its mother, aunts, sisters, grandmother and sub-adult males. Bond groups consisting of a few individuals will associate with other bond groups to form a clan. Most of the time, visitors see these bond groups or clans. It is only at certain times of the year you can see the so-called herds, such as at Minneriya, when a multitude of clans are drawn together by the need for food and water.

While a female will usually stay with her bond group when she grows up, males that have reached puberty are ejected by their family. These youngsters often roam in small bachelor groups, becoming more solitary as they grow older. Elephants continue to get bigger with age. An adult bull is significantly larger than an adult female, with a more sloping back and a bulge below the eyes which houses the base of its trunk. It also has a bigger trunk, which may reflect its use as a weapon when literally grappling for dominance with other males. Experience and size matter, and a male may have to wait until his mid-thirties before he can successfully mate with a female. Females use a number of visual, chemical and auditory clues to signal their readiness to mate.

Males in prime breeding condition exude a sticky fluid from a temporal gland near their ears. This is known as musth. During this time the males are pumped up with various hormones and can be quite aggressive. Generally a non-musth bull will give way to a musth bull. Young males that are not quite ready for an aggressive encounter with a more experienced bull have a subtle way of saying so: their musth fluid carries chemicals with a sweet odour, which signals that they are not a threat.

As recently as the mid 20th century, elephants were distributed all over Sri Lanka, up to the Horton Plains. Broadly speaking they are now almost confined to the dry lowlands, though a few small populations cling on in the wet lowlands. Human–elephant conflict has become a pressing conservation issue, and elephants are gradually becoming penned behind electric fences around protected areas. As the human population expands, the future looks bleak for Asia's largest terrestrial mammal.

Left Adult females are very protective of their young. (GSW)

Right Elephants enjoy frequent dust baths. (GSW)

A wild pig drinking keeps watch for lurking crocodiles. (GSW)

UNGULATES

In Sri Lanka, the even-toed ungulates in the order Artiodactyla fall into two suborders. The Suiformes (pigs and pig-like mammals) are represented by the family Suidae, with a single species, the wild pig. The Ruminantia (ruminants) are represented by three families: the Tragulidae, with two species of mouse-deer; the Cervidae, with four species of deer; and the Bovidae, with the Indian water buffalo.

WILD PIG

The wild pig is the ancestor of the domestic pig and, not surprisingly, shares many of its physical traits, including the elongated snout and short, thin tail. The young are hairy with longitudinal, white stripes. Males grow larger than females, with canine teeth that develop into tusks. The upper pair curves upward, with the bottom pair rubbing against them to maintain a sharp cutting edge. These tusks can grow up to 25cm long and are a formidable weapon. Males defend themselves fiercely, and even leopards are extremely wary of tackling a sounder (the collective term for pigs) that contains adult males.

Wild pigs are omnivorous, taking mostly vegetable matter, such as fruits, seeds and underground tubers, but also sometimes feeding from animal carcasses. They are found throughout the island, up to Horton Plains. In the lowland dry zone national parks wild pigs are often seen during the day, but elsewhere they tend to be more wary and nocturnal. They can survive in reduced forest long after other ungulates have been driven out.

Regular mud baths help pigs to remove parasites and keep cool. (GSW)

The sambar, Sri lanka's largest deer, is best seen at Horton Plains National Park. (UH)

DEER

There are four species of true deer found in Sri Lanka. The hog deer (*Axis porcinus*) is confined to a few swampy habitats on the southwest coast extending down to Galle; it is not clear whether this species is indigenous or introduced. The spotted deer is widespread in the dry lowlands, while the sambar and muntjac are widely distributed, both being found in the dry and wet zone lowlands, and in the highlands up to Horton Plains. The sambar is the largest of the deer and needs fairly large areas of forest cover. The much smaller muntjac occurs in smaller forest patches, usually surrounded by grassland and near streams or lakes. Wilpattu National Park is the best place to see this shy species, which is also known as barking deer on account of its calls.

The upper canines in male muntjacs have developed into short tusks. The antlers are on a long bony pedicel. In the other three species of deer the upper canines are

Only male spotted deer carry antlers. (GSW)

not well developed and the antlers are on a short pedicel. In all Sri Lanka's deer species – as with most deer – only the males have antlers. When growing, these are covered in a temporary skin filled with fine blood vessels, called 'velvet'. Once grown, the velvet dries and deer are sometimes seen rubbing off the dead skin. Males shed their antlers after mating. During the rut, they engage in duels to assert dominance in a herd – except for the muntjac, which live in pairs.

Deer have facial glands, which they rub against grasses and bushes in order to spread their scent. These glands are very pronounced in muntjac, for which scent marking is thought to play a stronger role in maintaining pair bonds and territories. Deer also have glands on their feet, which they use to deposit scent when making scrapes on ground, and may use dung middens to mark their territories.

Spotted deer are gregarious and form large herds in the dry lowlands national parks, sometimes numbering over a hundred. In protected areas such as at Yala and Wilpattu, they are active during the day, though elsewhere they are largely nocturnal. Sambar exist in low densities and are shy even in protected areas – with the exception of Horton Plains National Park, where large numbers gather on the plains in the late evening. This park has seen an explosion in the sambar population, due to increased protection and the spread of nutrient-rich grasses from the nearby Ambewela cattle farm. This has led to a rise in the population of leopards,

Predators take a heavy toll on fawns. (GSW)

whose main prey species in the highlands is sambar. In Yala National Park the leopard's main prey is spotted deer. Spotted deer have developed keen hearing, vision and smell to avoid predators, and are often seen in association with troops of hanuman langurs, which help provide yet more vigilant lookouts.

Muntjak deer are hard to see outside national parks. (GSW)

MOUSE-DEER

Mouse-deer are small, deer-like mammals in their own family, the Tragulidae. Neither sex has horns or antlers. Unlike other ruminants, which have a four-chambered stomach, a mouse-deer's stomach is three-chambered. These secretive animals are widespread across the country and may even be found in gardens with good cover.

Two species of mouse-deer are found in Sri Lanka: the white-spotted mouse-deer (*Moschiola meminna*) and the yellow-striped mouse-deer (*Moschiola kathygre*). The former is dull brown in colour and is larger than the latter, although size can be hard to judge in the field. It is found in the dry lowlands. The yellow-striped mouse-deer is a warm brown colour, with yellow, not white, spots and stripes. It is found in the wet lowlands and up to the mid hills, reaching the dry zone borders in some areas. The mouse-deer found in the highlands may represent a yet undescribed species.

Mouse-deer are herbivorous, feeding on the leaves of low bushes, grasses, fruits and berries. Being shy, solitary and nocturnal, they are rarely seen, though residents of areas around the Talangama Wetland and Bolgoda Lake, not far from Colombo, regularly report them in their gardens. Daytime sightings in the dry lowland parks are usually just a fleeting glimpse as the animal dashes across the road. Mouse-deer are reputedly able to run up low-angled, creeper-covered branches when pursued, thus making them the only ungulates in Sri Lanka that can climb trees. Apart from a chirping vocalisation, they are relatively quiet.

Cattle egrets enjoy rich pickings from insects disturbed by water buffaloes. (AS)

WATER BUFFALO *Bubalus bubalis*

The water buffalo is the only wild cattle species (subfamily Bovinae) found in Sri Lanka. It is not clear whether it was always present as a wild population, or whether it was introduced. Either way, there are now natural-living wild populations, although feral water buffalos continue to breed with these and much mixing of genes takes place.

Both male and female buffalos have permanent horns, though they lack the scent glands found on the face and feet of ungulates such as deer. They also have little hair, except for a terminal tuft on the tail. Their diet consists mostly of grasses and herbs, usually near water. Herds usually comprise adult cows with young and sub-adults. Bulls leave the herd on sexual maturity, only returning to mate.

Buffalos have poor eyesight, moderate hearing and a good sense of smell. Bulls often feed during the cool of the morning or evening, and are fond of wallowing in water when it is hot. They can be very aggressive and may attack unsuspecting walkers, sometimes fatally goring or trampling their victims. Indeed, buffalos are among the most dangerous of Sri Lanka's forest animals.

CARNIVORES

The order Carnivora embraces a variety of different animals, most of which live primarily by hunting other animals for food, although some also incorporate fruit and other items in their diet. These range from large powerful predators, such as big cats, to small squirrel-sized mongooses. All share a number of basic traits, including teeth and digestive systems that can handle meat, and forward-facing eyes that allow them to judge distance when pursuing prey. Carnivores in Sri Lanka are represented by a number of families, including the cats (Felidae), dogs (Canidae), bears (Ursidae), mongooses (Herpestidae), civets (Viverridae) and otters (Mustelidae).

LEOPARD *Panthera pardus*

The leopard is the largest of four cat species in Sr Lanka. This beautiful and enigmatic mammal is extremely widespread and adaptable, ranging from Indonesia to South Africa, and frequenting every habitat from deserts to snow-capped mountains. Sri Lanka's leopards constitute an endemic subspecies and are now largely confined to protected areas. The national parks of Yala and Wilpattu in the dry lowlands are the best places to see them, although they ascend up to the highlands and may also be encountered in Horton Plains National Park.

A leopard is about the size of a large dog, with a body about one metre in length and a tail nearly as long. Its yellow coat is beautifully patterned with distinctive black spots that form rosettes on the flanks. Males are distinctly bigger than females and can weigh up to 80kg. A black panther is actually a melanistic leopard, whose coat is rendered almost black because of a recessive gene. In Sri Lanka, black panthers are an extreme rarity, though regular reports of dark leopards from Sinharaja suggest that a darker form may have become more prevalent in the wet zone forests.

Because of their adaptability, stealth and cunning, leopards occur in habitats where even smaller cat species are not present – even in forest very close to human settlements. As recently as 2004, there were reports of leopards coming down at

Leopards are unique among big cats for their tree-climbing abilities, and can be very hard to spot among the dappled light of the foliage.
(GSW)

Power and grace epitomised (GSW)

Like those of all cats, leopard tracks show no claw marks. (GSW)

night to drink from Kandy Lake, in the heart of Kandy. Estate owners around the Roseneath Reservoir Forest Reserve also report regular sightings, as do residents of the nearby Hantane hills.

Block 1 of Yala National Park has one of the highest densities of leopards in the world, with up to one leopard per square kilometre. This figure should not be confused with home ranges: in Yala, an adult female will have a home range of $2–4km^2$, while an adult male may have a home range of $16–20km^2$, encompassing those of several females. The high density, relatively open terrain and the leopard's confidence as uncontested top predator combine to make Sri Lanka one of the best places in the world (and certainly the best in Asia) in which to photograph it.

At birth, leopard cubs of different sexes are nearly the same size. However, males grow up to be considerably larger than females. By 15 months, a sub-adult male is around the size of its mother, though it is still unable to fend for itself and relies on her for food. The mother may leave her cubs for several days at a time while she goes hunting, then summon them to a kill. When the cubs are repeatedly disturbed, for instance by vehicle traffic, she will move them to a new and hidden place, still within her home range.

Leopards generally hunt by stealth, getting as close to their victim as possible before launching a final charge or pounce. Prey ranges in size from small rodents to mammals as large as sambar. Their spotted coat reflects the dappled light of their forest habitat, allowing them both to conceal themselves when stalking prey and to hide their cubs from danger. Conversely the conspicuous white underside to the tail tip can work as a bold visual signal, allowing cubs to follow their mother.

SMALL CATS

Sri Lanka is also home to three smaller species of cat. Relatively little is known about these species and their behaviour, partly because they are all entirely

The secretive fishing cat is seldom seen. (GSW)

nocturnal. Most commonly seen is the jungle cat (*Felis chaus*), which is sometimes spotted in the evenings at Uda Walawe National Park. This species is larger than a domestic cat, slimly built and sandy grey in colour. It may be mistaken for a jackal at a distance. I have encountered jungle cats on public roads outside Yala National Park around midnight, after most vehicles have left. Like many cats, this species is largely solitary. Its distribution seems to be restricted to forest patches in the dry lowlands, though this may well reflect our relative ignorance of nocturnal mammals.

The rusty-spotted cat (*Felis rubiginosus*) is one of the smallest wild cats in the world.

The diminutive rusty-spotted cat is not uncommon in the dry lowlands. (PA)

At night it is easily confused with a small feral domestic cat, but can be distinguished by its reddish-brown coat, with a striped face and stripes along its body formed from elongated spots. The former wide range of this species may have shrunk considerably over the last century due to deforestation, but it still holds out in small forests in both the wet and dry zones. Daylight sightings are rare; I have seen it only very late at night on roads near national parks. It is reported to raid chicken coops and evidently is not averse to the presence of people, though has not recently been recorded around Colombo.

The fishing cat (*Felis viverrinus*) has a wide distrubution throughout the island. Its territory is linear, in that – like an otter – it occupies habitats alongside water bodies. An adult male can weigh 15kg and is a formidable predator. Its diet is mainly fish and freshwater molluscs, though it will also prey on birds and larger animals such as dogs. In other parts of the world, it has even taken small children. Fishing cats still inhabit the marshlands around Colombo, such as Talangama wetland and Kotte marshes, and urban areas with canals on the coastal road north also support good populations.

GOLDEN JACKAL *Canis aureus*

The golden jackal is Sri Lanka's only member of the dog family, and shares many traits with domestic dogs. It is found across southeastern Europe, southern Asia and the northern half of Africa. The race found in Sri Lanka is distinct from its counterparts on the Indian mainland, and is sometimes referred to as the black-backed jackal due to its dark back. However, this name is also used for a completely different African species, so to avoid confusion it is better to stick with the universally accepted names of golden or Asiatic jackal.

The social organisation of golden jackals is fascinating. They build monogamous ties, with a breeding pair establishing a territory and maintaining it through frequent scent marking and prominent dung middens. Pairs also howl together, often at night, to mark their territory. Studies in Africa have shown that golden

The golden jackal, like all dogs, follows its nose to find a meal. (GSW)

34

Golden jackals are versatile and intelligent animals. (GSW)

jackals direct their territorial aggression only towards members of the same sex. Thus a female will fend off another female and a male will fend off another male, acting alone. This action helps cement the monogamous pair bond. When the female comes into oestrus, the pair engages in many dominance interactions, with tails raised and much growling and whimpering. There may also be aggressive interactions with other members of the group.

Jackals are not true social animals that live and hunt in packs. They are, however, quite often seen in small groups. This is because the cubs of the previous year stay to assist their parents with the new litter. The helpers may not have attained sexual maturity yet, but even if they have, their ability to reproduce is suppressed by the dominant breeding pair. It is thought that in this way helpers gain experience that will be useful when they in turn turn become part of a breeding pair.

Jackals, like most dogs, bolt their food with minimal chewing. The meal may be regurgitated later, especially if they have pups or if a male is feeding his mate who is shortly to give birth. A pair will also regurgitate food for one another when one partner has failed to get its fill. Sometimes they will tear a carcass in two and feed separately a short distance apart, ensuring that at least part of their meal can be saved if a larger predator steals the rest of it.

Contrary to popular belief, scavenging provides a relatively small part of jackals' diets. They also hunt small animals, and occasionally the young of larger mammals, and will take fruits to supplement their otherwise carnivorous diet. Their preference for small prey can bring them into conflict with poultry farmers, and local children's stories abound with stories of the wily jackal and the poultry farmer. This conflict is, however, not serious enough to warrant any action to control them.

Golden jackals are found right across Sri Lanka, ascending up to the mid hills, but they are most common in the scrub jungles of the dry zone where prey is more abundant. Their intelligence and ability to adapt to a purely nocturnal lifestyle has enabled them to live near man. Jackals are still found in the Muthurajawela Wetland, a few kilometres from the international airport at Katunayake, north of Colombo.

Sloth bear, Yala (GSW)

SLOTH BEAR *Melursus ursinus*

The sloth bear is the only bear species found in Sri Lanka. The race on the island is endemic, although in the field it is not distinct from the Indian race. Like all bears, it has a stocky build, thick hair and plantigrade feet – ie: the soles make complete contact with the ground when walking, as in humans. Females are smaller than males, with thicker fur on their back. This helps them carry their cubs, which 'piggy back' on their mothers when they are very young.

Like all bears, the sloth bear is omnivorous, its diet varying somewhat according to seasonal availability of food. It eats a variety of vegetable matter, including the flowers of the mee tree, and will gorge itself on the sweet, intoxicating fruit of the palu tree during May and June. It will also scavenge on fresh kills throughout the year. However, perhaps the most notable feature of the sloth bear's diet is termites, and to this end it seems to be evolving into something of a specialist. Adaptations include an elongated palette, protrusible lips and two missing front teeth, which allow it to blow away dust and sand, and suck in termites. Termites are a more important part of its diet during the wet season, when it can use its long powerful claws to rip open termite mounds.

Sloth bears are primarily nocturnal, which means that they are generally hard to see, even though there may be plenty around. In Wasgomuwa National Park, for example, average densities may be as high as one per square kilometre. In Yala, there may be fewer, but they are more tolerant of humans and daytime sightings are possible. Sloth bears are absent from the wet zone.

Sloth bears will scavenge from a carcass when the opportunity arises. (Luxshmanan Nadaraja/Studio Times)

Sloth bears do not appear to be markedly territorial, and individuals wander widely. Game drives in Yala for example, will sometimes encounter an individual over 20km away from where it was seen the previous day. Battle wounds, such as a torn ear, help to identify each individual. Though the bears tend to forage alone by day, they are known to sleep communally.

Unfortunately the sloth bear is one of the most feared animals of Sri Lanka's forests. Sudden encounters may cause a bear to charge – especially a female protecting her young – and a mauling may inflict terrible injuries. Locals, especially the Vedda people, have traditionally carried an axe and a wooden stave to ward off attacks. However, a sloth bear will usually retreat when it hears a person or if you shout at it. Attacks are brief: the sloth bear is not attempting to kill or eat its victim, merely to defend itself. Opinion is divided as to whether you should stand your ground or run away to safety. Rangers I have spoken to often advise the best course of action with a charging sloth bear is to run away if its charge is not stopped by a shout. This advice does not apply to other species of bear elsewhere, especially the large ones that may make predatory attacks on a human.

CIVETS, MONGOOSES AND OTHER CARNIVORES

The ruddy mongoose (*top* GSW) is smaller than the more boldly marked stripe-necked mongoose (*above* GSW)

Civets and palm-civets are sometimes misleadingly known as civet-cats or palm-cats, though they are not cats at all. In fact, they belong to the family Viverridae, and are more closely related to mongooses, which in turn make up the family Herpestidae. These two families of small carnivores are considered to be among the most primitive of their order, with similar species known from fossil records dating back to the lower Oligocene.

Civets and palm-civets have elongated bodies, a pointed muzzle, short legs and a long tail. Their feet have five toes, with claws that are retractable to varying degrees. Many species have pre-anal glands, from which they can secrete a strong-smelling fluid. Three species occur in Sri Lanka, all of which are nocturnal. The widespread small civet (*Viverricula indica*), also known as the ring-tailed civet is easy to identify, with its black and white body and 'ring-tail'. It is a terrestrial mammal, often encountered on roads at night, including in urban areas, and sometimes visiting houses to take food – though not taking up residence in the manner of the palm-civet. The common palm-civet (*Paradoxorus hermaphroditus*) and endemic golden palm-civet (*Paradoxorus zeylonensis*) belong to a different subfamily and are both arboreal. The former is dark in colour and fond of residing in the lofts of houses, where its pungent urine makes it an unwelcome tenant. It is often seen bounding across and between roofs. The latter is an overall golden-brownish colour. It is a forest animal, occuring mainly in the lowlands and mid hills of the wet zone.

The common palm-civet often finds a home in roofs. (GSW)

Mongooses are generally smaller than civets, with small, round ears, and are more terrestrial in their habits. Four species are found in Sri Lanka: the brown mongoose (*Herpestes fuscus*), the ruddy mongoose (*Herpestes smithii*), the grey mongoose (*Herpestes edwardsi*) and the stripe-necked or badger mongoose (*Herpestes vitticollis*). It is possible for a visitor to see all of these during a two-week tour of the island.

The grey mongoose is common in the northern half, but scarce in the south where it is replaced by the ruddy mongoose. Around the cultural sites in the North Central Province, this species is often seen dashing across a road into cover, and can quickly be identified by its overall grey colour and small size. The ruddy mongoose is a grizzled brown and has a characteristic habit of carrying its black-tipped tail curled up. It is reasonably confiding in protected areas such as Yala National Park. The brown mongoose lacks the black tip to the tail and carries it straight. It is widely distributed in both the lowlands and the highlands, though at a lower density than the grey and ruddy mongooses. It can be seen during the day, but is more nocturnal in its habits. The stripe-necked mongoose is the largest species and has a beautiful coat. Its wide distribution includes the highlands up to Horton Plains, though it occurs everywhere in naturally low numbers. It is probably the most self-confident of the mongooses, and a pair foraging for grubs in a protected area like Yala can be very tolerant of safari jeeps.

Another widespread carnivore is the otter (*Lutra lutra*), which belongs to the weasel family, or Mustelidae. This shy, fish-eating mammal is widespread across the island and is the same species as found in Europe, readily identified by its broad muzzle, tapering tail and short-legged stature. It is an expert swimmer, using its muscular tail and webbed feet to power it along. Stories abound of otters raiding private ponds and cleaning out the fish overnight. Though generally nocturnal, they sometimes visit the lake at Hunas Falls Hotel near Kandy in broad daylight; I have had several fleeting daytime sightings there.

PRIMATES

Primates are the most intelligent and evolved order of mammals. They are divided into two suborders: the Prosimii (*prosimians*) comprises the more primitive lemurs, lorises, galagos and tasiers; the Anthropoidea comprises the monkeys, apes and humans. Both are represented in Sri Lanka, the former by two species of loris (*Loris* spp.) and the latter by three species of monkey. Together these five species represent a fair cross-section of the primate evolutionary tree, and they occur at unusually high densities.

LORISES

Lorises are among the most ancient of primates. Sri Lanka has two species, the grey loris (*Loris lydekkerianus*) and the red loris (*Loris tardigradus*). The grey loris is present in good numbers in the North Central Province, around Sigiriya and Polonnaruwa. The red loris occurs mostly in the wet zone lowlands. Two separate highland races, one found in Horton Plains National Park and one in the Knuckles range, may yet be classified as separate species.

Lorises are small mammals that could fit inside a pair of cupped hands. They do not have tails, and their forward-facing, saucer-like eyes are more reminiscent of an owl than a monkey. Both species are agile animals that move nimbly within trees – the red loris being smaller and more active. Their acute sense of smell is important in marking territories and signalling their readiness to breed. They also use a special claw on one digit of each hand, called the 'toilet claw', for scratching and cleaning out their ears, and a modified tooth with comb-like serrations, for general grooming.

Although lorises use a range of vocalisations, a short shrill whistle – easily mistaken for an insect's call – is generally all that is heard by humans. This and their unobtrusive, nocturnal behaviour may explain why people are often not aware of their presence.

MONKEYS

Sri Lanka's three monkey species all belong to the family Cercopithecoidea, or old world monkeys. This can be futher divided into two sub-families: the Colobinae includes the langurs and colobus species; the Cercopithecinae has the baboons, macaques and guenons. Sri Lanka's endemic purple-faced leaf monkey (*Presbytis senex*) and hanuman langur (*Presbytis entellus*) belong to the former. The endemic toque macaque (*Macaca sinica*) belongs to the latter.

The grey loris is strictly nocturnal. (KN)

Purple-faced leaf monkey (UH)

The southern race of the purple-faced leaf monkey shows a pale back and tail. (UH)

Leaf monkeys are long-tailed monkeys that live in the trees, where they eat mostly leaves. The purple-faced leaf monkey has two races in the wet lowlands, one to the north of the Kalu Ganga (river) and one to the south of it. The western race (the one to the north) is found in places such as the Talangama Wetland, around Bellanwila Attidiya and Lake Bolgoda. It is critically endangered, mainly due to loss of habitat. The southern race (to the south of the river) can be seen in Sinharaja Rainforest. It has a prominent white patch on its rump and side of the rear legs. The tail is frosted white. Another race in the highlands, known as bear monkey, has a shaggy coat to offer protection from the cold.

The other leaf monkey, the graceful hanuman langur, has long limbs, a pale grey-brown coat and a dark face. Long eyelashes help it to avoid the glare when feeding in treetops. Generally leaf monkeys are shy and not likely to trouble people. But at least one habituated population of hanuman langurs has shown aggression, and this usually inoffensive animal can be a formidable sight when gnashing its fearsome incisors.

The toque macaque – or toque monkey – is more compact and shorter-tailed than leaf monkeys, and more terrestrial in its habits. It has reddish- to yellowish-brown fur, and cheek pouches that contain salivary compounds for breaking down toxins in its plant food. These pouches, absent in leaf monkeys, also help it to deal with feeding competition by literally stuffing faces. Sri Lanka's pronounced climate zones have resulted in three races of the toque macaque, with one in the dry lowlands, one in the wet lowlands and one longer-haired race in the highlands.

Most cheek-pouch monkeys maintain male-dominated hierarchies with an alpha male. However, studies of toque macaques show that the troops are formed on matrilineal lines, with females providing the stable core. This species is hierarchical and the young of higher-placed females inherit a higher status in the troop. Toque macaques are widespread in Sri Lanka and can be common in some populous areas. They should always be treated with caution – especially where people feed them, which gives them the impression that humans are subordinate.

Right Female hanuman langurs are very protective of their young. At times the young may gather into a small crèche. (GSW)

Below Toque monkeys maintain close-knit family bonds, which they reinforce with regular grooming. (GSW)

WHERE TO WATCH PRIMATES IN SRI LANKA

Sri Lanka offers outstanding opportunities to observe primates at close quarters. The following are among the best sites.

Talangama Wetland

The Talangama Wetland is a 30–45-minute drive from central Colombo, where most of the tourist accommodation is based. It is a reliable location in which to see the critically endangered western race of the purple-faced leaf monkey.

Hakgala Botanical Gardens

The Hakgala Botanical Gardens are 15–20 minutes' drive from the highland town of Nuwara Eliya. Above them is the Hakgala Strict Nature Reserve, a refuge for rare montane plants and animals. The montane races of the purple-faced leaf monkey, shy elsewhere, and the toque macaque are used to people here and so easily observed.

Udawattakale, Kandy

The forbidden forest of the ancient Kandyan kings is on a hill behind the famous Temple of the Tooth Relic, which overlooks the Kandy Lake. The wet zone race of the toque macaque, known as the dusky toque, reigns supreme here, in large quarrelsome troops. Don't feed them: this will only encourage aggression.

Sigiriya and Polonnaruwa archaeological reserves

These popular archaeological sites in the North Central Province are surprisingly rich in primates, with the dry lowland race of the toque macaque, the northern race of the purple-faced leaf monkey and the hanuman langur all occuring in troops together. The hanuman langurs and toque macaques are both quite bold; the latter will steal your sandwiches, given half a chance. This area is also very good for the nocturnal grey loris.

The rainforests of Galle

Kottawa, Hiyare and Kanneliya are rainforests that can be reached from Galle: Kottawa and Hiyare are within half an hour's drive; Kanneliya one-and-a-half hours away. The southern race of the purple-faced leaf monkey occurs in small shy troops. The nocturnal and endemic red loris also lives here, but is hard to find.

Purple-faced leaf monkey
(highland race) (GSW)

The giant squirrel can become quite confiding, especially at feeding tables. (GSW)

SQUIRRELS

Squirrels are rodents (order Rodentia), which account for more species than any other order of mammal in Sri Lanka except bats. The majority of rodents, including rats, mice and gerbils (see page 49), are small, nocturnal and hard to identify. Squirrels, however, are both conspicuous and endearing, and more easily identified by the casual visitor. Like all rodents, they have a pair of powerful, chisel-like incisors in both the upper and lower jaw.

Sri Lanka has six species of squirrel. These include two nocturnal species of flying squirrel: the giant or grey flying squirrel (*Petaurista petaurista*) and the small flying squirrel (*Petinomys fuscocapillus*). The grey flying squirrel is about one metre long, of which half is tail. The small flying squirrel is about 60cm long, with the tail again being about half its total length. But colour can be an easier distinguishing feature in the field: the grey flying squirrel looks black (despite its name); the small flying squirrel is rufous-chestnut – though bear in mind that some torches can make an animal look even redder.

Flying squirrels have membranes of skin along their flanks that connect their forelegs to their hindlegs. During a glide, they stretch these out like a sail and have

Giant flying squirrels use their long tails for balance when airborne. (GSW)

been known to cover more than 30m. They also have long bushy tails, just like other squirrels, which gives them balance and control while gliding – much as a cheetah uses its long tail during a high-speed chase. Flying squirrels have developed an acute sense of smell to help them find food at night.

Both flying squirrels are seldom seen, more on account of their nocturnal habits than being scarce. The giant flying squirrel is less shy than the small, and at times takes up residence near houses in tea estates or other plantations that still have a mix of old, native trees. The Hotel Tree of Life at Yahalatenna near Kandy is a good site. Both species nest in a tree hole, unlike diurnal squirrels which construct a domed nest or 'drey'.

The most common of the diurnal squirrels is the palm squirrel (*Funambulus palmarum*). It is divided into four geographic races based on differences in colouration, especially of the stripes on its back. Palm squirrels are abundant in towns and home gardens. Unlike other mammals, they are very vocal, with a loud, bird-like 'chink chink' call, which they repeat constantly throughout the day. Town dwellers with a tree-filled garden will often have palm squirrels as dominant members of the dawn chorus. The call seems to demarcate territories as well as to maintain contact between a

Every garden seems to have a pair of palm squirrels. (GSW)

pair. Territories can be quite small in food-rich gardens: an acre of land can hold up to eight pairs in a leafy suburban area.

Palm squirrels also have an interesting association with yellow-billed babblers (see page 53). The latter have a tight-knit social organisation, with the flock helping a dominant pair to breed. Each flock of yellow-billed babblers seems to associate with a pair of palm squirrels. It is likely that both squirrels and babblers benefit from having more eyes to look out for predators. The babblers may also snap up insects disturbed by the squirrels' feeding, while the squirrels' alarm call may help to warn them of predators such as domestic cats.

The flame-striped or Layard's squirrel (*Funambulus layardi*) is around the size of the palm squirrel. It is greyish-black in colour, with a prominent orange-coloured stripe running along its spine, but can look darker in the dense shade of the wet zone rainforest where it lives. Taxonomists have recently recognised this species as endemic to Sri Lanka. The diminutive dusky squirrel (*Funambulus sublineatus*) also occurs in the wet zone rainforests, and enters parks, gardens and golf courses in the highland town of Nuwara Eliya, close to the cloudforest of the Mount Pedro range. This species has three stripes that are slightly paler than its chocolate brown upperparts. Both the Layard's and the dusky squirrel are wary of people. In the rainforest they tend to follow mixed-species feeding flocks of birds – the dusky often betraying its presence with an occasional high-pitched bird-like 'chink'.

The giant squirrel (*Ratufa macroura*) is around 80cm long, with the tail making up about half of this length. Its size alone easily separates it from the other squirrels. It has three fairly distinct subspecies: the two wet zone forms of the lowlands and highlands are superficially similar, with the upperparts a deep black and the underparts yellow; the dry zone form is a uniform sandy colour. This species can become a confident visitor to hotel restaurants in a wilderness setting, where it readily accepts offerings of food. Unlike the palm squirrel, however, it does not seem able to adapt to an urban environment, and is never far from areas with tall forest.

BATS

Of the 89 species of terrestrial mammal recorded in Sri Lanka, no fewer than 31 are bats. Very little is still known about many of them and it is possible that new species of this fascinating, nocturnal group still await discovery.

Bats have a number of unique adaptations. First, and most obvious, they are the only mammals capable of true flight, as opposed to gliding. Their long curving forearms have evolved into wings, supporting a membrane of skin that extends from the tip of the forearm digits to the back legs and usually encompasses the tail, too. To ensure a low body weight, bats' legs are extremely light, and so not robust enough to support their weight for long. Bats therefore sleep upside down, which has brought other evolutionary changes to their internal organs and blood circulatory systems. Bats are also famous for using echolocation – bouncing high-frequency sounds off their surroundings in order to navigate and capture prey. They are not the only mammals to do this; many cetaceans (see page 119) use the same technique, but the earliest studies of echolocation were based on bats. All bats are most active after dark. During the day they usually sleep quietly in a shaded place in a cave or tree.

The Indian flying fox is the largest and most conspicuous of the island's bats. (GSW)

The short-nosed fruit bat (*top* UH) is the smallest of the fruit bats. Leaf-nosed bats (*above* UH) feed on insects caught in flight.

The bats belong in the order Chiroptera. This is split into two suborders, the Microchiroptera, with roughly 750 species around the world, and the Megachiroptera, with roughly 150 species. Broadly speaking, the former eat insects and the latter eat fruit.

Three species of fruit bat are found in Sri Lanka. These are the Indian flying-fox (*Pteropus giganteus*), the dog-faced bat (*Rousettus seminudus*) and the Indian short-nosed fruit bat (*Cynopterus sphinx*). Fruit bats utter calls, but few use echolocation. Instead they rely on good sight and a sense of smell to find food. Flying-foxes have a wingspan of up to 1.3m, and are the biggest and best known of Sri Lanka's bats. They form large roosts in public open spaces and sometimes besides main roads. These can have complex social interactions: at times, only members of the same sex may roost together. The dog-nosed bat roosts communally in dark caves. Like flying-foxes, it is a noisy animal that can be heard some distance from the roost. This species uses its eyesight in open habitats, but in dark caves and forests it switches to echolocation.

The Microchiroptera are divided into seventeen families or sub-families. The exact divisions between these are a matter of taxonomic debate, but it is generally accepted that Sri Lanka has eight families or sub-familes: tomb bats (Emballonuridae), false vampire bats (Megadermatidae), leaf-nosed bats (Hipposiderosidae), horse-shoe bats (Rhinolophidae), tube-nosed bats (Murininae), painted bats (Kerivoulinae), long-fingered bats (Miniopterinae) and free-tailed bats (Molossidae).

Most Microchiropterans feed on insects taken on the wing or picked off the ground. The elaborate 'leaf' or tragus on the nose of many species enhances their echolocation powers when pursuing this elusive prey. The false vampire bats (Megedermatidae) also take larger, vertebrate prey such as geckos and skinks. Each species has its own distinctive flight pattern and a preferred height at which it flies. One of the best ways to identify bats – indeed, often the only way in the field – is by using a bat detector, which converts their high frequency calls outside the range of human hearing into a range that is audible to people.

OTHER MAMMALS

In this book it is not possible to cover in detail all the smaller mammals of Sri Lanka, most of which a visitor is unlikely to encounter. However, a few more are worth a brief mention here.

The black-naped hare (*Lepus nigricollis*) is often spotted at night on public roads. However, in national parks such as Yala, daylight sightings are also possible. This species is widely distributed thoughout the island and even manages to hold out in the suburbs of Colombo. Many carnivores, from wild cats to ring-tailed civet, prey on hares, which breed in prolific numbers to sustain their populations in the face of intense predation.

The porcupine (*Hystrix indica*) is a large nocturnal rodent, covered in long black-and-white spines, that is widespread across the island. It even holds out in the suburbs of cities, where it is sometimes seen by day. Porcupines feed on a wide variety of plant matter, from leaves to fruit, and can plunder rich pickings from suburban gardens.

Top The black-naped hare, though generally nocturnal, is often sighted by day in Yala. (Devaka Seneviratne/Studio Times)

Above The pangolin is widespread, but very seldom seen. (GSW)

The pangolin (*Manis crassicaudata*) has a patchy distribution across the island up to the mid hills. This bizarre-looking animal has a scaly body, with a long tail, powerful claws for ripping open termite hills and a long tongue for picking out its termite food. Pangolins may not be as rare as one might imagine from the rarity of sightings, though sadly they are often poached for meat.

One of the commonest rodents in the dry lowlands is the antelope rat (*Tatera indica*), which can be distinguished from other rats in Sri Lanka by its fully furred tail with a black tuft at the tip. The Indian bandicoot (*Bandicota indica*) is a stoutly built rather fearsome-looking rat that frequents forest habitats. It has adapted readily to gardens, where it makes itself a nuisance by digging up plants to feed on tubers.

Shrews look superficially similar to rats and mice but in fact belong to an altogether different order, the Insectivora. They eat insects, as their name suggests, whereas rodents feed mainly on plant matter. The house-shrew or common musk-shrew (*Suncus murinus*) is spread throughout the island and can be encountered in urban dwellings. It is about 15cm long, greyish in colour and can be distinguished from a mouse by its pointed snout. The pygmy shrew (*Suncus etruscus*) is 5cm long and is the island's smallest mammal. It has been recorded widely but seems to have its stronghold in the highlands. Most shrews live less than two years.

WATCHING NOCTURNAL WILDLIFE

A host of mammals are most active at night. This includes common animals, such as the black-naped hare, unusual creatures such as pangolin and porcupine, and otherwise elusive small carnivores such as small civet and rusty-spotted cat. In the dry zone, leopards, jackals and jungle cats will be out hunting, while prey animals such as sambar, wild pig and deer are also more likely to be active. Elephants, too, often feed at this time, while primate enthusiasts can look for lorises.

Night-time often reveals a richness of wildlife that you could not have imagined during daylight hours. Even a site such as Talangama Wetland on the outskirts of Colombo can produce small civet, fishing cat, porcupine, yellow-

Brown fish owl (GSW)

striped mouse-deer, black-naped hare and brown mongoose. And it is not only mammals that come out at night. The rewards of a nocturnal walk or drive may include insects, such as moths, and reptiles, such as geckos, that feed on them. Hunting the small rodents and reptiles will be snakes – and nocturnal birds, including owls and nightjars, which have evolved silent flight and powerful sensory equipment for hunting in the dark. The brown fish owl (*Ketupa zeylonensis*) is a spectacular owl that can tolerate people and feeds almost entirely on fish.

For viewing nocturnal mammals it is best to take a head-mounted torch or else to hold a torch as close as possible along the trajectory between one's eyes and the subject. This way you can best see an animal's 'eye shine'. White light will often dazzle animals or cause them to flee. But animals don't mind red light, so try using a torch with a red filter or even a piece of red cellophane wrapped around the front. Avoid torches with LED bulbs, as these may damage an animal's retina – and never point a light directly at an animal, which can leave it confused and alarmed.

In Sri Lanka, visitors – even most researchers – have to exit national parks by dusk. Therefore most nocturnal encounters by visitors will be on their way back to their hotel after an evening game drive. Anti-poaching legislation may result in some rangers attempting to prosecute people spotlighting animals. It is therefore a good idea not to be prowling within a designated national park or reserve at night. If you use a red filter and explain that you are mammal watching, rangers may assist you to look for mammals on public roads outside park boundaries. If in doubt, ask: help is usually forthcoming.

BIRDS

Serendib scops owl (UH)

In the 14th century, Marco Polo described Sri Lanka as the finest island of its size in the world. Birdwatchers today are likely to agree, albeit for different reasons. The island's complex mosaic of habitats boasts one of the highest densities of bird species in the world. No fewer than 446 species have been recorded on the island, of which 230 are resident. Most significant among these are the 33 species that are endemic – ie: can be seen nowhere else on earth.

Every year huge numbers of migrants arrive to swell the ranks of the residents – scientists estimate more than a million birds in total. They start to arrive from August, though greater numbers come in September and October. The majority hail from Europe, and northern and central Asia. These travellers are believed to follow one of two key routes. The western route originates to the northwest of the Himalayas and follows the west coast of India. Large numbers of wintering ducks, follow this route. The eastern route brings birds from Siberia and Mongolia, down through Tibet and along the east coast of India. Large numbers of waders, such as little stints, follow this route, as do passerines such as the barn swallow, brown shrike and forest wagtail. These two routes form part of what is known as the 'central Asian flyway'. A handful of southeast Asian species, such as the black-capped kingfisher, also visit Sri Lanka. Their route is still unclear, though some scientists have suggested that it may pass through the Andaman Islands.

Loten's sunbird uses its long bill to probe flowers for nectar. (GSW)

BIRDS OF TOWN AND GARDEN

A small garden in the heart of a city in Sri Lanka, with a good mix of fruit trees and flowering plants, can feel like a private nature reserve. Its most dazzling residents are the sunbirds, which feed on nectar and have taken a liking to many introduced flowering plants. The smallest is the purple-rumped sunbird (*Nectarinia zeylonica*), with the male having a green crown and brownish wings. The male Loten's sunbird (*Nectarinia lotenia*) has a long down-curved beak and glossy purplish upperparts. In the dry zone it is replaced by the purple sunbird (*Nectarinia asiatica*), which has a shorter beak and a blackish, not brown, belly.

In the canopy are the colourful fruit-eating barbets. The brown-headed barbet (*Megalaima zeylanica*) is the biggest, about half the size of a crow, with a green body and a brown head.

The rose-ringed parakeet has been declared a pest for its raids on paddy fields. (GSW)

It uses its powerful beak for excavating nest holes, as well as for hacking through the thick hides of fruits such as jak (*Artocarpus heterophyllus*). The diminutive Ceylon small barbet (*Megalaima rubricapilla*), only the size of a sparrow, also visits gardens if they have tall trees. Another fruit-eater is the pale-billed flowerpecker (*Dicaeum erythrorhynchos*). This diminutive greyish bird, the smallest on the island, is fond of visiting jam trees (*Muntingia calabura*) for their fruit.

No small town garden seems complete without a pair of magpie robins (*Copsychus saularis*). These black-and-white birds are beautiful songsters. Another garden favourite is the yellow-billed babbler (*Turdoides affinis*). This drab-looking bird is always busy and sociable, travelling in little flocks that keep up a constant chatter mixed with bouts of hysteria at the approach of a neighbour's cat.

High on the glamour stakes is the black-headed oriole (*Oriolus xanthornus*), whose colourful black and yellow plumage is matched by a repertoire of beautiful liquid vocalisations. Usually seen in pairs, these are birds of the tree canopy. Ring-necked parakeets (*Psittacula krameri*), with their bright green plumage and red bills, are also increasingly visiting gardens where birdseed is put out for them.

Hunters include the greater coucal or crow pheasant (*Centropus sinensis*), with its black head and neck, and rufous upperparts. This bird is actually related to cuckoos, but uses its powerful bill to hunt for insects and small vertebrates on the ground. Another handsome hunter is the widespread brahminy kite (*Haliastur indus*), with its striking combination of white head and rufous wings. It is often seen soaring over towns. A smaller bird of prey, the shikra (*Accipiter badius*), likes heavily wooded gardens, where it uses cover to dash after small birds. By night, collared scops owls (*Otus bakkamoena*) and brown hawk owls (*Ninox scutulata*) are enigmatic hunters. The latter is the size of a crow and finds televison antennas a convenient perch. The smaller scops owl prefers wooded thickets.

A number of migrant birds also visit gardens. Every town in Sri Lanka receives its share of blue-tailed bee-eaters (*Merops philippinus*), which breed in India. These colourful birds like to perch on high vantage points, such as television antennas, from where they dart out to snap up insects in flight. Another aerial insect-catcher is the barn swallow (*Hirundo rustica*). Flocks of these agile birds, with their elegant tail streamers, can be seen hawking over towns soon after their arrival, before gradually spreading out into the open countryside. Sometimes hundreds perch together on telephone wires.

Down at ground level, the Indian pitta (*Pitta brachyura*) takes up residence in dense undergrowth in gardens and forests throughout the island. Many arrive in central Colombo, moving out to the suburbs after they have regained their strength. This ground-dwelling species breeds in the Himalayan foothills and central India. Despite the dazzling blue on its wings and tail, it is very unobtrusive. The forest wagtail (*Dendronanthus indicus*) is another species that spends its time searching for insects, grubs and worms on the forest floor. This active little bird, with its distinctive double breast-band, breeds in northeastern Asia (across China). It prefers heavily shaded forest patches, but sometimes turns up in gardens in central Colombo.

Top The blue-tailed bee-eater is a common migrant, even to cities. (GSW)

Above The male Asian paradise flycatcher develops long tail streamers. (Studio Times)

Sri Lanka is also an extremely important destination for many species that breed in the Himalayas. Most notable is the Kashmir flycatcher (*Ficedula subrubra*), which may have almost its entire population wintering in Sri Lanka's highlands – though some also settle in the mid-hills, where Victoria Park in Nuwara Eliya is a well-known site. Males have distinctive robin-like red underparts. Its Himalayan relative, the Asian brown flycatcher (*Muscicapa dauurica*), occupies the tree canopy in wooded gardens throughout the island. The orange-headed thrush (*Zoothera citrina citrina*) is easily identified by its bright orange head and underparts. This bird may stop over in gardens, even in busy towns, though most head to the lowlands, hills and forest patches.

The Asian paradise flycatcher (*Terpsiphone paradisi paradisi*) is one of Sri Lanka's more spectacular garden birds. The resident race (*T. p. ceylonensis*) is joined in winter by migrants of a separate race (*T. p. paradisi*) that breeds in India. By their second year, males of this race have developed the long tail feathers characteristic of the species, but their plumage remains red – like that of the resident race. By the third year, however, males of the Indian race have begun to turn white. Females of the two races are similar. Migrant birds disperse widely in the lowlands, preferring forested hills and well-wooded gardens, and often join mixed-species feeding flocks in the wet zone forests.

One of Sri Lanka's most conspicuous migrants is the brown shrike (*Lanius cristatus*), which spreads across the island and settles wherever scrubby habitats are present. Its loud chattering calls and habit of perching on top of a bush draw attention, and at times every bush in Yala seems to have one. Brown shrikes often take up residence near cemeteries and golf courses. They breed in central Asia, eastwards to Korea.

BIRDS OF THE RAINFOREST

Nowhere are Sri Lanka's avian riches more obvious than in the lowland rainforest of Sinharaja, an essential site for birdwatchers. This area has become famous for the mixed-species feeding flocks that, since 1981, have been the subject of one of the longest-running projects of its kind anywhere in the world.

The first clue to the presence of a feeding flock is an audible one – often either the constant medley of squeaks and chatters from Ceylon rufous babblers (*Turdoides rufescens*) or the far-carrying bell call of a crested drongo (*Dicrurus lophorinus*). The latter is a fearless bird that serves as sentinel to the flock and will ward off attacks from birds of prey, such as a goshawk (*Accipiter trivirgatus*) or serpent eagle (*Spilornis cheela*). Meanwhile, in the dark undergrowth below, flocks of ashy-headed laughingthrushes (*Garrulax cinereifrons*) are betrayed by their calls. Every good feeding flock also has its dark-fronted babblers (*Rhopocichla atriceps*) – looking like surprised bandits, with their white eye and dark mask – and a pair of black-naped monarchs (*Hypothymis azurea*). Interestingly, research has shown that both these species have fixed territories, but join up with the flock for a while as it passes through their space.

The crested drongo is an accomplished mimic of other birds. (GSW)

Yellow-fronted barbet (GSW)

In the tall canopy, yellow-fronted barbets (*Megalaima flavifrons*) and Layard's parakeets (*Psittacula calthropae*) forage for fruit. A sharp call may alert you to the endangered white-faced starling. Gorgeous Ceylon blue magpies (*Urocissa ornata*) comb the forest in small flocks, looking like a child's painting in their livery of chocolate brown, red and blue. Atop endemic rattans are Ceylon hanging-parrots (*Loriculus beryllinus*), time-sharing their perches with Legge's flowerpeckers (*Dicaeum vincens*). Ceylon hill-mynas (*Gracula ptilogenys*), common here, fill the air with their noisy calls, competing with the drumming of the barbets and the screeching of the parakeets. In contrast the red-faced malkoha (*Phaenicophaeus pyrrhocephalus*) stays silent, except for an occasional grunt. Birders may see a dozen in a day at Sinharaja or it may elude them completely.

The male Malabar trogon (*Harpactes fasciatus*) is a gorgeous bird with a striking red breast and wings finely barred in black and white. The female is relatively drab. Pairs are often encountered in the feeding flocks. The oriental dwarf kingfisher (*Ceyx erithacus*) is a small, sparrow-sized forest kingfisher that is more often heard than seen. Despite colourful orange underparts and a hint of crimson, it is easily overlooked for one of the many bright-coloured forest leaves. Black bulbuls (*Hypsipetes leucocephalus*) are dark birds with an orangish red bill and legs. They draw attention by being quite raucous.

A rainforest birding itinerary should also take in Kithulgala, for a second chance of malkoha as well as the strange troll-like Ceylon frogmouth (*Urocissa ornata*). The latter, a sub-continental endemic, is also found at Bodhinagala, about 90 minutes from Colombo. This patch of secondary forest, set around a small temple, is also famous for the green-billed coucal (*Centropus chlororhynchos*), another shy endemic. Sinharaja, Kithulgala and Morapitiya are good sites for this bird, too. These four areas may all afford a glimpse of the extremely shy Ceylon spurfowl (*Galloperdix bicalcarata*), whose loud series of descending and ascending notes is often heard, even if the bird remains hidden. In contrast, the spot-winged thrush sings sweetly and is relatively easy to see.

The Ceylon frogmouth (*top* UH) and red-faced malkoha (*above* GSW) are both elusive denizens of dense rainforest.

BIRDS OF THE HIGHLANDS

No garden in the highlands seems to be without a flock of endemic Ceylon white-eyes (*Zosterops ceylonensis*) and endemic yellow-eared bulbuls (*Pycnonotus penicillatus*).

The Ceylon white-eye is bigger and darker than the oriental white-eye, which is common in the lowlands. The white eye-ring is distinctive. Yellow-eared bulbuls are loud, handsome birds with a black-and-white face and prominent yellow ear coverts. They visit trees and shrubs and feed on small fruits. More discreet is a third highland endemic, the dusky blue flycatcher (*Eumyias sordidus*). This small powder-blue bird can become quite confiding, and may take up residence in gardens with a suitable wooded edge. The Indian blackbird (*Turdus simillimus*) has a striking orange-red bill and ring around the eye. This is generally a shy forest bird, which ventures onto roads and forest paths at dawn or dusk

The forests around the highland town of Nuwara Eliya hold leopard, but birdwatchers are often happy to settle for Sri Lanka bush-warbler (*Elaphrornis palliseri*) or, if extremely lucky, a Ceylon whistling-thrush (*Myophonus blighi*). For the latter, the best site is Arrenga Pool in Horton Plains National Park. A pre-dawn departure is required for the 45-minute journey from Nuwara Eliya to this precious remnant of cloudforest interspersed with grassland. A visit to Arrenga Pool may also yield Ceylon whistling-thrush, as well as Ceylon wood pigeon (*Columba torringtonii*) and perhaps even a scaly thrush (*Zoothera imbricata*). Pied thrushes (*Zoothera wardii*) and otters (*Lutra lutra*) occasionally visit the pool, too. In the evening, large herds of sambar (*Cervus unicolour*) emerge from the forest to graze, attracting their key predator, the leopard.

Top Yellow-eared bulbul (GSW)

Above Ceylon wood pigeon (GSW)

The northern winter brings its bounty of visitors, with the forest flocks joined by chestnut-winged cuckoos (*Clamator coromandus*), brown flycatchers (*Muscicapa dauurica*) and Indian paradise flycatchers (*Terpsiphone paradisi paradisi*), with their long white tails. Some migrants hold a special appeal for birders. Victoria Park, in the highland city of Nuwara Eliya, has become a draw for the Himalayan specialities that take up residence: a flock of pied thrushes are ever present, while Indian blue robins (*Luscinia brunnea*) join Indian pittas (*Pitta brachyura*) to forage on leaf litter. The entire population of the threatened Kashmir flycatcher (*Ficedula subrubra*) is believed to winter in Sri Lanka and Victoria Park, or even the Nuwara Eliya golf course, always holds a few.

An added bonus of the hill regions is the cultural attractions. Birding itineraries usually pass through the hill capital of Kandy, famous for its spectacular pageant in July and August, with richly decorated elephants. The Temple of the Tooth is one of the most revered Buddhist temples and birders usually fit in a short cultural visit to this particular Kandyan temple.

Kashmir flycatcher (GSW)

BIRDS OF THE DRY LOWLANDS

From the cool highlands, the roads wind down to the dry lowlands. Here, too, birders can search for migrants in Bundala National Park, the Palatupana Salt Pans or Yala National Park. In these places, visitors can get astonishingly close to migrant waders, sometimes in their thousands. At Palatupana, curlew sandpipers (*Calidris ferruginea*), waders with long down-curved bills, gather in large flocks to probe the mud. Joining them are often greater sand plovers (*Charadrius leschenaultii*) and lesser sand plovers (*Charadrius mongolus*), two very similar dumpy-headed waders with sandy brown plumage.

There are also a number of interesting resident species. The yellow-wattled lapwing (*Vanellus malabaricus*) is an arid zone specialist, with distinctive yellow wattles on its face. The Indian stone-curlew's (*Burhinus indicus*)

Yellow-wattled lapwing (GSW)

Top Great thick-knee (GSW)

Above Crested hawk eagle (UH)

cryptic camouflage plumage is easily overlooked, but the plainer plumage of its relative the great thick-knee (*Esacus recurvirostris*) is easier to spot, and this bird seems less fussed about concealment. A night drive should yield both Jerdon's (*Caprimulgus atripennis*) and Indian nightjars (*Caprimulgus indicus*). These two species look very similar to the untrained eye and are best distinguished by call. The town of Tissamaharama provides an access point to the national parks and some of the many ancient manmade lakes that dot the country and provide good wetland habitat. It offers plenty of accommodation for birdwatchers.

When the migrants are in, a day's birding in Yala or Ruhunu national parks can yield more than 100 species. Malabar pied hornbills (*Anthracoceros coronatus*) fly laboriously overhead, while blue-faced (*Phaenicophaeus viridirostris*) and sirkeer malkohas (*Taccocua leschenaultii*) withdraw hastily. The blue-faced malkoha is is very agile at threading its way through small trees, usually offering just a brief glimpse of a darkish, long-tailed bird with white on the tail. The sirkeer malkoha is more of a ground-dwelling cuckoo, whose red bill and red legs contrast with its plain brown plumage.

Both Yala and Uda Walawe national parks are particularly good for raptors. These include the crested serpent eagle (*Spilornis cheela*), whose dark brown plumage is relieved by some spotting on the mantle and yellow at the base of the bill. This species spends long periods sitting quietly, searching for prey on the ground below. The similar sized crested hawk eagle (*Spizaetus cirrhatus*) always lacks the yellow at the base of the bill. The shaheen falcon (*Falco peregrinus*) is a dark race of the peregrine falcon, which has a worldwide distribution, and has chestnut underparts and slaty upperparts. The famous archaeological site of Sigiriya usually has a pair catching the thermals.

The dry lowlands are steeped in a 2,300-year continuous tradition of Buddhism.

The crested serpent eagle is an expert catcher of snakes, which it swallows whole. (Studio Times)

In the North Central Plains lies the city of Anuradhapura, the island's capital from the 3rd century BC to the 10th century AD. In remarkably good condition, thanks to modern restoration with UNESCO support, are the world's largest brick structures, the stupas (also known as *cheityas* in Sri Lanka). Polonnaruwa, which succeeded Anuradhapura as the capital from the 10th to 15th century, was also a sprawling metropolis, which saw a renaissance in art. These archaeological reserves often serve a twin purpose as nature reserves and some are of special interest to birders. A fine example is the rock citadel of Sigiriya, the residence of the mad artist king Kasyappa, where birders may find orange-headed thrush and watch little swifts (*Apus affinis*) circle over the lofty palace, dodging the shaheen falcons. At night, as elephants emerge from the scrub forests, spot-bellied eagle owls and Jerdon's nightjars begin their hunting.

The black-necked stork is the largest of Sri Lanka's storks. (GSW)

BIRDS OF THE WETLANDS

Sri Lanka is blessed with many natural wetlands, several thousand manmade lakes and thousands of hectares of rice paddies. Not surprisingly it supports a wealth of resident wetland birds. Amongst the most visible are herons and egrets. The pond heron (*Ardeola grayii*) and cattle egret (*Bubulcus coromandus*) are familar birds on roadside rice fields. The former is cryptically patterned with brown streaking above, but flashes striking snow-white wings in flight. The cattle egret, as the name suggests, is closely asociated with cattle and indeed the two creatures enjoy a symbiotic relationship, the egrets keeping a lookout for the grazing bovines who in turn flush out a supply of insects for the birds. The cattle egret's yellow bill and chunky body separate it readily from the little egret (*Egretta garzetta*), which has a fine black bill and yellow feet, and prefers to hunt fish in water. When the paddy fields are being ploughed, all egret species, together with pond herons, flock to feast on the invertebrates and amphibians that are exposed. The statuesque purple

62

The lesser adjutant is internationally endangered. (GSW)

heron (*Ardea purpurea*) does not join these muddy forays, preferring to hunt in marshlands. In the dry lowlands, the grey heron (*Ardea cinerea*) is more common than the purple heron.

Every roadside telephone wire in Sri Lanka next to a paddy field seems to have a white-throated kingfisher (*Halcyon smyrnensis*), whose chocolate-coloured and white underparts contrast with its blue upperparts. This species feeds mainly on insects and amphibians. The common kingfisher (*Alcedo atthis*), however, lives up to its name better by catching only fish. This species is familiar to birdwatchers in Europe and, with its orange underparts and dazzling blue upperparts, is an undeniably beautiful bird.

Crotchety and garrulous are the purple swamphens (*Porphyrio porphyrio*), bedecked in blue, with bright red bill and legs. Mewing and adding to the wetland cacophony is the pheasant-tailed jacana (*Hydrophasianus chirurgus*), with breeding adults sporting a golden nape and long tail streamers. The cotton teal (*Nettapus coromandelianus*) is elegantly patterned in black and white and, though widespread in

Little egrets pursue fish energetically through the shallows. (GSW)

the lowlands, this dainty little duck is always thin in numbers. A more common resident is the lesser whistling-duck (*Dendrocygna javanica*), which utters a characteristic whistling call in flight.

Migrant waterfowl visit Sri Lanka's wetlands in great numbers, and certain wetland sites, such as Bundala National Park, have received Ramsar status (following the wetlands conservation convention signed at the Iranian town of that name) due to their international importance. Wetland habitats include paddy fields and marshes, and many are easily accessible from towns. Residents of Colombo, for example, can see a wealth of migrant waterbirds by visiting Talangama, Kotte Marshes or Bellanwila Attidiya.

Among ducks, the most abundant migrant is the garganey (*Anas querquedula*), which arrives from Europe and Asia to settle on freshwater lakes, especially in the dry lowlands. Like all ducks, it wears its breeding plumage during the winter mating season. After breeding, males assume their non-breeding plumage, known as eclipse, which looks like the females' except for a bluish-grey patch on the upper wing.

The black bittern (*Dupetor flavicollis*) is a skulking member of the heron

The common kingfisher catches small fish by plunge diving from a perch. (GSW)

family, which frequents lowland swamps and marshes. Sri Lanka's resident population is boosted each year by an influx of migrants, probably from India and China. The glossy ibis (*Plegadis falcinellus*) feeds more in the open, using its long, curved bill to probe for invertebrates. A few migrant individuals settle each year in Sri Lanka's wetlands and mangrove areas.

A variety of waders migrate to different various wetland habitats across the island. The black-winged stilt (*Himantopus himantopus*), easily identified by its exceptionally long legs, is resident in the dry lowlands, but almost entirely absent from the wet zone outside the migration season. The pintail snipe (*Gallinago stenura*), by contrast, has shortish legs but an extremely long bill. This cryptically camouflaged species visits paddy fields and marshes in the lowlands, where upon arrival it may be less skulking than usual, often appearing on the embankments of paddy fields, looking somewhat bewildered. It breeds north of the Himalayas.

Other waders include the lesser sand plover (*Charadrius mongolus*), which breeds in central Asia. This forms large flocks on migration, which gather in open, short-cropped grasslands in the dry lowlands and appear in greater numbers near the coast. Small flocks of the slightly larger Pacific golden plover (*Pluvialis fulva*) also visit wet pastures and short-cropped grasslands in the lowlands. This species breeds in northern Siberia. The marsh sandpiper (*Tringa stagnatilis*) is a medium-sized wader, quickly identified by its pale colouring, pencil-thin bill and slender build. Individuals occur in lowland wetlands. On arrival, they stop over on freshly ploughed paddy fields. This species breeds in southern Russia and central Asia. The smaller common sandpiper (*Actitis hypoleucos*) visits the same habitats, but can also be seen along

Male purple swamphens often come to blows over territorial rights. (GSW)

The black-winged stilt (*above left* GSW) and marsh sandpiper (*above right* GSW) are widespread waders of lowland wetlands.

streams and canals anywhere in the country. Look out for its stiff-winged flight and white 'finger' marking around the bend of the folded wing. Common sandpipers breed across northern Europe and Asia.

BIRDS OF THE COAST

Being an island with several hundred kilometres of shoreline, Sri Lanka enjoys a good tally of seabirds. However, one of the most spectacular annual seabird events is very little known. Every August there is a huge southward movement of seabirds along the west coast, including a few hundred thousand bridled terns (*Sterna anaethetus*), as well as Wilson's petrels (*Oceanites oceanicus*) and various species of skuas and other terns. The migrants can be picked out from around Chilaw past Colombo,

The Caspian tern has the biggest bill of any tern species. (Studio Times)

and then seem to swing further out to sea before Galle. As much of this movement takes place at least a kilometre offshore, it goes largely un-noticed. Much of what we know is due to the work of Rex de Silva, a dedicated seabird watcher who has spent over two decades documenting it.

On Adam's Bridge, the string of islets loosely connecting the island of Mannar with the Indian mainland, thousands of little terns (*Sterna albifrons*), lesser crested terns (*Thalasseus bengalensis*) and great crested terns (*Thalasseus bergii*) breed.

Security considerations mean these islands are not easy to visit. In July, the rocks off Ambalangoda in the south also hold large flocks of great crested terns.

Most of the seabirds encountered in Sri Lanka are migrants. Species regularly seen on the shoreline include the gull-billed tern (*Gelochelidon nilotica*), which acquires a smart black cap in breeding plumage. The whiskered tern (*Chlidonias hybrida*) and white-winged tern (*Chlidonias leucopterus*) are winter visitors that prefer inland fresh waters. The common tern (*Sterna hirundo*), lesser-crested and great-crested terns are sea-going species rarely seen inland, unless roosting on an estuary. The Caspian tern (*Hydroprogne caspia*) is the biggest of its kind, with a haunting cry and a powerful orange beak.

Wading birds flock to the inter-tidal zone, where they find a wealth of food. Each species has its own specialisation: the sanderling (*Calidris alba*), for instance, races up and down the beach between waves, snapping up tiny crabs, shrimps and other crustaceans. This tiny wader is symbolic of the shoreline. The much larger whimbrel (*Numenius phaeopus*) feeds on larger crabs, and uses its longer bill to probe deeply for worms. It prefers estuarine habitats, whilst the larger and longer-billed Eurasian curlew (*Numenius arquata*) likes salt marshes. Most species of wader prefer the edges of brackish waters in lagoons and estuaries. They feed on the rich feast of invertebrates in the mud. Many, however, can turn up on the coastline for brief periods. I have even watched pond herons (*Ardeola grayii*), typically a bird of freshwater wetlands, hunting crabs on the coastline.

Sanderlings are found on undisturbed sandy beaches all around the island. (GSW)

ENDEMIC BIRDS

Sri Lanka is famed among birdwatchers for its high number of endemic species. To see all 33, you must combine a visit to a lowland rainforest with a trip to the highlands. A trip to Sinharaja will produce most, but not Ceylon bush warbler or Ceylon whistling-thrush. Thus you will also need to visit Horton Plains to complete your list. Nonetheless, if you have time to visit only one birdwatching site in Sri Lanka, Sinharaja should be it.

The following list briefly outlines Sri Lanka's endemic birds. It follows the taxonomic order used by Rasmussen in the *Ripley Guide to the Birds of South Asia*, which is similar to that of most field guides.

Ceylon spurfowl *Galloperdix bicalcarata*

Extremely shy. Found in pairs in wet zone forests and riverine forests in the dry zones. Loud duetting betrays their presence, though birds often remain well hidden. Notoriously elusive and wary, even at Sinharaja. Looks like a female junglefowl, but has black and white belly markings in both sexes.

Ceylon junglefowl *Gallus lafayetii*

Widespread up to the mountains in surviving forest tracts. Best seen in the dry zone national parks, especially early in the morning. Extremely nervous in the wet zone forests, except in protected forests where it is habituated to handouts. The female is brown with barred wings. The male, with his golden neck, resembles a domestic cockerel.

Ceylon wood pigeon *Columba torringtonii*

Prefers large forested stretches in the highlands, but makes seasonal movements to the lower hills, descending as low as Sinharaja. Generally likes well-forested areas, although may visit gardens. It has a bluish-grey body with a black-and-white marking on the hind neck. Larger than a feral pigeon.

Ceylon green-pigeon *Treron pompadora*

Male has a conspicuous purple mantle. Female is similar to the orange-breasted green-pigeon, but with a greenish rather then grey nape. Found throughout the island, but less common than orange-breasted. A great traveller and may even turn up in the suburbs.

Top Ceylon junglefowl (GSW)

Above Ceylon hanging parrot (GSW)

Ceylon hanging parrot *Loriculus beryllinus*
Quite common in the wet zone up to the mid-hills, occuring locally in riverine forests in the dry zone and in some dry zone areas such as Gal Oya. A small, green bird with a red crown (in the male) and beak. Often seen hurtling overhead, uttering a three-syllable call.

Layard's parakeet *Psittacula calthropae*
Found in and around good-quality wet zone forest in the lowlands and mid hills. Sometimes also in dry zone areas such as at Gal Oya. Flocks wheel around, calling noisily. Female has a dark bill. Also called emerald-collared parakeet, although this feature is not always clear in the field. Distinctive raucous call.

Green-billed coucal
Centropus chlororhynchos
Found only in a few lowland rainforests such as Sinharaja, Morapitiya and Kithulgala. A few birds also occur in small pockets such as Bodhinagala. Probably one of Sri Lanka's most endangered birds. Very similar to the greater coucal, which is a common town and garden bird. The green, not black, bill is diagnostic.

Red-faced malkoha
Phaenicophaeus pyrrhocephalus
Confined to a few remaining tall forests in the lowland rainforests, including Sinharaja, Morapitiya and Kithulgala, where almost always seen with mixed-species feeding flocks. Generally silent, but occasionally utters a guttural croak. In Sinharaja, now habituated to people. Striking, yet hard to see in the canopy.

Green-billed coucal (GSW)

Combination of red face, black upperparts and white underparts and tail is unmistakable.

Serendib scops owl *Otus hoffmanni*
First seen in 2001 and described to science in 2004. Reddish-hued plumage and soft single-note call helps prevent confusion with other scops owls. Male has orangish irides (the 'whites' of a bird's eye); female's are yellowish. Overall reddish-brown plumage and apparent lack of ear-tufts help separate it from the other two scops owls. Restricted to a few lowland rainforest areas such as Sinharaja and Kithulgala, where generally seen at the disturbed forest edge, often near the ground.

Chestnut-backed owlet *Glaucidium castanonotum*
Found in well-wooded areas in wet zone lowlands and hills. Probably more common than is popularly realised. Diurnal, but would easily escape notice were it not for its wide repertoire of calls. Chestnut upperparts, with head finely barred in grey and white.

Ceylon grey hornbill *Ocyceros gingalensis*

Female has dark mandibles with a yellow 'island' along the middle. Male has yellow mandibles with a dark patch at the base. Widespread, occuring in almost every sizeable forest patch in the lowlands and hills. Utters a series of rolling calls and a harsh, far-carrying 'kraaa'. Overall grey upperparts and lack of a casque on the upper mandible make confusion with the larger Malabar pied hornbill unlikely.

Yellow-fronted barbet *Megalaima flavifrons*

Found mainly in the wet zone lowlands and hills. Displaces brown-headed barbet in heavy forest. A common bird in the gardens and tea estates of the mid-hills and highlands. Like all barbets, the body is green. It has a yellow forehead and blue on the face.

Ceylon small barbet *Megalaima rubricapillus*

'Pop pop pop' calls uttered from a high vantage point help locate this sparrow-sized bird. Found in gardens and forests in the lowlands and hills, also in the heart of cities such as Colombo and Kandy. Easily overlooked due to its small size and arboreal nature. Like all barbets, loves to feed on ripening figs. It has yellow around the eyes and a crimson forehead. Lacks the streaking on the underparts found in the similar coppersmith barbet, which replaces it in the dry zone.

Crimson-backed flameback
(GSW)

Crimson-backed flameback *Chrysocolaptes stricklandi*

Found in well-wooded gardens and forests in wet-zone lowlands and hills. Displaces the commoner black-rumped flameback in dense forest patches. Utters a shrill whinnying call when flying from one tree to another. The 'red-backed' form of the more common black-rumped flameback is similar, but the crimson-backed has an ivory-coloured bill. Female's crown is black with white flecks.

Ceylon swallow *Hirundo hyperythra*

Deep red underparts and rump help separate this from the migrant races of the red-rumped swallow, which may also have clear streaking on the underparts. Found throughout the island, often hawking insects over open areas. Red underparts separate it from the migrant barn swallow, which also has blue uperparts.

Ceylon wood-shrike *Tephrodornis affinis*

Found mainly in the scrub jungle of the dry lowlands. Not uncommon in suitable forests and adjoining *chena* (slash-and-burn agriculture) lands with patches of scrub forest. Sexes are similar. A nondescript bird: greyish overall, with pale underparts and a dark mask.

Ceylon grey hornbill (GSW)

Ceylon wood-shrike (GSW)

Black-capped bulbul *Pycnonotus melanicterus*

Occurs mainly in the wet zone forests in the lowlands and hills. Also locally present in some dry zone forests. Black cap and yellow plumage are distinctive. Shows white-tipped tail feathers in flight.

Yellow-eared bulbul *Pycnonotus penicillatus*

Look for this bulbul in the wet zone hills and highlands. Most common in the highlands, where it often visits gardens. Face is strikingly patterned in black and white with yellow ear-tufts. Calls strongly.

Spot-winged thrush *Zoothera spiloptera*

Superb song betrays its presence in many forests in the wet lowland and hills. Common in damp forests, where it forages for invertebrates on the forest floor. Not rare, but long-term survival depends on the future of wet zone forests. White spots on the wings are easy to make out if you have a good view. The face is marked strongly in black and white.

Ceylon scaly thrush *Zoothera imbricata*

Like the spot-winged thrush, found in wet zone forests from the lowlands to the highlands. Partial to forest patches adjoining streams. Heavier bill than spot-winged thrush, with plumage scaled rather than spotted and hissing call more high-pitched. Discreet; seldom sings.

Spot-winged thrush (GSW)

Ceylon whistling-thrush *Myophonus blighi*

Male is brownish-black, with a blue gloss on the fore parts and a blue shoulder patch. Female is brown with a blue shoulder patch. Best located early in the morning or late in the evening by shrill grating call. Confined to the cloudforests in the central highlands and the Knuckles.

Dusky blue flycatcher *Eumyias sordidus*

A forest bird of the highlands, found occasionally in the mid hills. Has adapted to human presence and will visit gardens. May be mistaken for the black-naped monarch, but has blue, not white, belly and under-tail coverts, and its behaviour is less frenetic.

Ashy-headed laughingthrush *Garrulax cinereifrons*

Confined to a few extensive lowland rainforests. Prefers to forage near the ground and occasionally at the shrub layer, almost always in mixed-species feeding flocks. Flocks keep up a medley of 'hysterical'-sounding calls, sometimes with a faint metallic quality. Extremely timid, always keeping within cover and fleeing in haste across any road it meets. The 'Barrier Gate' flock at Sinharaja offers a good chance to see this bird. It has an ashy head and brown body.

Brown-capped babbler
Pellorneum fuscocapillus

A small brown babbler with a darker brown cap. Skulking, rarely showing itself in the open. Presence betrayed by distinctive 'pritee dear, pritee dear' call. Found throughout the island up to the highlands, wherever forest patches remain.

Ceylon scimitar babbler
Pomatorhinus [schisticeps] melanurus

Lives in forested areas all over the island. Separate dry zone and wet zone races have been described, but are indistinguishable in the field. Almost always found in a duetting pair: male utters a long

Brown-capped babbler (GSW)

bubbling series of calls that ends with a 'kriek' from the female. So well synchronised that sound often appears to come from a single bird. Prominent white 'eyebrow' and the down-curved 'scimitar' bill are diagnostic.

Ceylon rufous babbler *Turdoides rufescens*

Always found in noisy flocks, and is a nucleus species of mixed-species feeding flocks. Usually seen in the wet zone rainforests, mainly in the lowlands but also in the highlands, and tends to occur only where extensive, undisturbed forests remain. Almost absent from the heavily disturbed Kanneliya Rainforest. Orange bill and legs, rufous body and constant chattering help separate it from other bablers.

Ceylon bush warbler *Elaphrornis palliseri*

A dark skulking warbler that keeps close to the forest floor. Found in *Strobilanthes* thickets in the highland forests, such as those around Nuwara Eliya. Pairs keep in touch using a series of contact calls. Both sexes have a reddish-brown wings and tail. Male has reddish irides; female's are pale.

Legge's flowerpecker *Dicaeum vincens*

Prefers tall forests in the lowland wet zone, where often seen quite close to the ground when feeding on the ripe berries of the common *Osbeckia* species along roadsides. Male sings from a high perch. Distinguished from other flowerpeckers by blue upperparts, white chin and throat, and yellow belly. Female is duller.

Ceylon white-eye (GSW)

Ceylon white-eye *Zosterops ceylonensis*

A clear 'split' in the white eye-ring, in front of the eye, helps distinguish this species from the oriental white-eye. It is also darker and slightly larger. The calls of the two species are very different. Found mainly in the highlands, but makes occasional seasonal movements to the lowland wet zone where it mixes with the oriental white-eye. Flocks of small green birds in highlands gardens are of this bird.

White-faced starling *Sturnia albofrontata*

Restricted to a few lowland wet zone forests, where it frequents the canopy, often joining mixed-species feeding flocks. Its sharp calls are the best clue to its presence. It has greyish upperparts, paler streaked underparts and a white face and pale bill. Tends to keep to the canopy, but may come down lower to feed on the fruit of shrubs such as bowitiya (*Clidemia hirta*) and *Osbeckia* spp.

Ceylon hill-myna *Gracula ptilogenys*

Found in the lowland wet zone forests, where it keeps to the high canopy. Utters a range of high-pitched, far-carrying calls and whistles. Distinguished from the lesser hill-myna by having one pair of wattles, not two, and a black base to bill. Both species show a lot of white on the wing in flight.

Ceylon crested drongo *Dicrurus lophorhinus*

Restricted to wet zone forests, from the lowlands to mid elevations. Deeply forked tail is normally without rackets (the projections on the outer tail feathers found in

Ceylon blue magpie (GSW)

many drongos), but may occasionally show rackets and can then be confused with the greater racket-tailed drongo of dry zone riverine forests. A tuft-like projection on the forehead is visible at close quarters. Has a lovely repertoire of belling calls and is a great mimic.

Ceylon blue magpie *Urocissa ornata*

Hard to believe this unbelievably colourful bird belongs to the crow family! Chocolate brown on the head and wings, with a red bill, eye-ring and legs set against blue plumage with white on the tail. Always found in small flocks, which will participate in helping a pair to nest and raise young. Restricted to substantial areas of wet zone forest.

REPTILES AND AMPHIBIANS

Land monitor (AS)

R eptiles are a class of vertebrates descended from amphibians and closely related to birds – which, in turn, are believed to have descended from them. They have dry skin covered in scales and are popularly described as 'cold blooded'. In fact, their body temperature varies with their surroundings – as opposed to that of warm-blooded animals (mammals and birds) which maintain a fairly constant temperature through internal, metabolic processes. Snakes and a few burrowing lizard species have lost their limbs, but most other reptiles have four legs.

Reptiles are divided into four orders, of which three occur in Sri Lanka. The Chelonia, or tortoises and turtles, comprise two species of freshwater turtle, one tortoise and five nesting marine turtles. The Crocodylia comprise two species of crocodile. The Squamata, comprise 46 species of lizards in the suborder Sauria and 95 species of snake in the suborder Serpentes. The rate of endemism in this last order is very high, with 18 endemic agamid lizards, 14 endemic geckos and a remarkable 43 endemic snakes.

LIZARDS
Sri Lanka has six families of lizard. Five are commonly encountered by the visitor and these are described here. They are: the monitors (Varanidae); the Agamid lizards (Agamidae); the geckos (Gekkonidae); the skinks (Scincidae); and one chameleon (Chamaelonidae).

MONITORS
Monitors – sometimes known locally as iguanas – are extremely large lizards, with powerful limbs, loose skin covered in bead-like scales and tiny tongues that they flick in and out, like snakes, to test the air. The water monitor can exceed 2m in length, including its long, powerful tail. Two species occur in Sri Lanka: the land monitor (*Varanus bengalensis*) is widespread throughout the lowlands, and seemingly equally comfortable in the northern and southern halves of the island; the water monitor (*Varanus salvator*), by contrast, is absent from a line south of the Nilawala River. The young of both are heavily marked in yellow, which fades with age. The adults of

Water monitors play a useful role as scavengers. Their appetite for snakes makes them popular.
(Nihal Fernando/Studio Times)

the two species are quite easy to tell apart, as the adult land monitor is uniformly ash-coloured, while the water monitor retains its markings.

The water monitor is the bolder of the two species, largely because a belief that its flesh is poisonous has left it untroubled by hunting. It likes marshy habitats, where it will slip away into the water when threatened. When cornered, this lizard can inflict fearsome injuries by lashing its tail at an assailant. Its wide diet includes birds, eggs and other reptiles, and it will prey on snake species that are fatally venomous to people. A boat ride in the Muthurajawela Wetland provides good viewing of water monitors, and they are often encountered on walks in the Talangama Wetland or in the Bellanwila Attidiya Sanctuary on the outskirts of Colombo. I have more than once been startled when a sizeable individual has dashed away suddenly from its camouflaged position beside a footpath.

The land monitor, by contrast, is a more wary animal – perhaps because its meat is considered tasty and similar to poultry. However, in places where they are not hunted, such as hotels with large gardens, these big lizards can become quite bold. From time to time an individual takes up residence in my garden in Colombo and happily forages during the day, oblivious to the presence of people.

AGAMID LIZARDS

Sri Lanka has 18 species of agamid. These are generally solid, medium-sized lizards, many of them sporting bright colours, flaps, spines or crests. Some live mainly in trees, though they are also perfectly at home on the ground. Many are endangered due to loss of habitat.

The best-known and most abundant agamid in Sri Lanka is the common garden lizard (*Calotes versicolour*), which is found up to an altitude of around 1,000m. It frequents scrub and, as the name suggests, is often encountered in gardens – usually seen running up a tree trunk. The green garden lizard (*Calotes calotes*) is the largest agamid. It is found throughout the lowlands to an altitude of 1,500m, but is more common in the wet zone. This species may also be seen in city gardens. The male has white transverse stripes on a green body and its head turns a bright crimson when displaying.

The green garden lizard is a common urban resident. (GSW)

The sand lizard, or fan-throat lizard, (*Sitana ponticeraiana*) is found in dry areas in the lowlands – especially in coastal areas with sand dunes and scrub edges. The male extends a showy gular (throat) sac when displaying. The black-lipped lizard (*Calotes nigrilabris*) is an endemic found at altitudes above 1,000m. It prefers montane forests but can also be seen in disturbed areas. Horton Plains National Park is a reliable spot for this species, and there is a well-known colony in the grounds of St Andrew's

Territorial conflict between common garden lizards often breaks out into fights. (GSW)

Hotel in Nuwara Eliya. The kangaroo lizard (*Otocryptis weigmanni*) gets its name from its habit of running bipedally when the occasion demands. It can also make powerful leaps, several times its body length, to evade danger. It is found in the lowlands, especially in rainforests in the wet zone. The black-dewlap lizard (*Otocryptis nigristigma*) prefers the dry zone, and can be distinguished from the kangaroo lizard by a distinct black patch on the sides of the mature male's dewlap – the loose fold of skin found around his neck.

Some Sri Lankan agamids are confined to relatively tiny areas, typically in the mountains. One of the most interesting is the dwarf lizard (*Cophotis ceylanica*), which occurs at heights of above 1,300m. This species has recently become scarcer, perhaps

due to a gradual drying of its cloudforest habitat. It has two unusual adaptations: firstly a prehensile tail, and secondly the ability to give birth to live young by a process known as ovo-viviparity (which is akin to hatching the egg inside the body rather than laying it). The latter is believed to be an adaptation against the cold climate.

Another lizard of the moss-covered cloudforest is the rhino-horned lizard (*Cerataphora stoddarti*), which is found above 1,200m. The exact function of the male's nose horn is a mystery, although scientists as early as Darwin have speculated that it may serve as an indicator of sexual fitness.

The endemic rhino-horned lizard is confined to the highlands (UH)

The maculate lizard (*Calotes desilvai*) was described from specimens collected in Morningside Forest. It differs from the similar and more widespread whistling lizard (*Calotes liolepis*) by the distinct black stripes on the throat. The crestless lizard (*Calotes liocephalus*) is restricted to the Knuckles, where it came under threat from the clearing of the undergrowth for cardamon cultivation. This practice was banned after the upper reaches of the Knuckles were declared a conservation area. Other endangered lizards of the cloudforest include the leaf-nosed lizard (*Ceratophora tennenti*), which is restricted to the Knuckles, and Erdelen's lizard (*Cerataphora erdelini*) and Karu's lizard (*Ceratophora karu*), both confined to eastern Sinharaja.

The rough-nosed lizard (*Ceratophora aspera*), the smallest of the agamids, is a ground-dwelling species that is found in relatively undisturbed patches of

The whistling lizard likes to stay on trees above head height and is easily overlooked. (UH)

lowland rainforest. Visitors to Galle can look for it in the nearby Kottawa Arboretum and Rainforest. The hump-nosed lizard (*Lyriocephalus scutatus*) is found in densely shaded forests below 1,650m. It is one of the largest and most striking of the agamids, with a pronounced lyre-shaped head and a bright green colouration – though the gular sac can take on shades of blue during displays. It is usually found on trees, but is also often observed on bare trunks close to the ground. The painted-lip lizard (*Calotes ceylonensis*) inhabits dry evergreen forests in the lowlands. It was recently found in Yala National Park, which suggests its distribution may be wider than previously thought.

GECKOS

Geckos are among the reptiles most familiar to people in the tropics, with almost every house having its coterie of resident individuals. They also exist in a wide variety of other habitats, from arid areas to humid rainforests, and many species are entirely nocturnal. Their ability to change the pattern and colour of their skin makes geckos hard to tell apart, and the ones found in houses actually comprise several different species.

The Gekkonidae as a whole are characterised by their large, unblinking eyes and soft skin. The undersoles of their feet have fine membranes that allow them to cling to smooth and vertical surfaces using surface tension. They are mainly

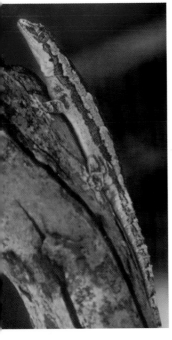

The bark gecko is diurnal and employs camouflage to avoid detection. (GSW)

insectivorous, usually lying in wait for an insect to come within striking range – often, in the case of house geckos, even including their own species. They are also known to eat other geckos and may even engage in cannibalism. Like some other reptiles, geckos can shed their tail, leaving a predator to cope with the flailing appendage while the former owner makes its escape.

The geckos of Sri Lanka have not been studied fully and half a dozen new species have been described to science in recent years. Currently there are thought to be 25 species on the island, of which 14 are endemic. The two most common are the Brooke's house gecko (*Hemidactylus brooki*), an endemic, and the common house gecko (*Hemidactylus frenatus*). The former has a rough skin and a flattened body. The latter is pale and smooth skinned, and has a call of three or four notes. According to local superstition, it is not auspicious to leave a house if a gecko calls.

The termite-hill gecko (*Hemidactylus triedrus*) is a common species found within tree hollows and termite mounds in the dry zone. The bark gecko (*Hemidactylus leschenaultii*) can be found on small trees or in houses. It can grow to nearly 9cm in length and it is known to eat common house geckos. The genus Cnemaspis contains several small species, many of which are diurnally active, hence their colloquial name of day geckos.

A few species of gecko that live in houses have benefited from human development and have spread their range by being inadvertently transported. Most forest species, however, are at risk from habitat loss and the impact of insecticides and pesticides. Their natural predators include snakes and birds, but domestic cats also take their toll.

The spotted house gecko is one of several species commonly found inside buildings. It plays a useful role in the household by feeding on insect pests. (GSW)

The spotted skink is widespread in the lowlands, where it can be seen foraging in leaf litter. Skinks often bask on rocks when the sun is up. (UH)

SKINKS

Sri Lanka has at least 30 species of skink, with several waiting to be named as new species, and probably several more waiting to be discovered. They are quite distinct from the agamids, being short legged and usually dark in colour above, and tend to forage on leaf litter. Most are quite shy and quick to move away. However, they can be reluctant to abandon a good sunbathing spot until you approach too close. Visitors are most likely to encounter species of *Mabuya* skink. The common skink (*Mabuya carinata*) is found everywhere from gardens to forests and, at around 12cm, is the largest species. It is stoutly built, and coloured dark above with pale longitudinal stripes. Around rocky outcrops, especially in the dry lowlands, visitors may also see the rock skink (*Mabuya macularia*). From the front of its head to the middle of the back it is a shiny gold, with a black stripe along the flanks. Some species of skink are fossorial, living mainly underground. Little is known about these species in Sri Lanka.

CHAMELEONS

The common garden lizard is often erroneously referred to as a chameleon. But the true chameleon found in Sri Lanka is the Sri Lanka chameleon (*Chamaeleo zeylanicus*), which occurs predominantly in the dry northern half of the island. Despite its name, this reptile is not endemic. However, it is scarce and seldom seen, trusting to its camouflage to escape notice. Like chameleons elsewhere, it has a number of characteristics that are unique among lizards. It can rotate each eye independently, has opposable fingers and toes, and uses its prehensile tail as a fifth limb – for example for grasping branches. Chameleons feed mainly on insects, which they catch by shooting out their sticky tongue.

SNAKES

Snakes are closely related to lizards. The most obvious difference between the two is that snakes do not have limbs or eyelids, although neither do certain species of lizard. All snakes are predators. The diet varies from invertebrates in some smaller species to vertebrates as large as deer in the case of the huge python.

Snakes show a number of unusual adaptations. Without limbs, they cannot tear up their prey into smaller pieces. However, a hinged jaw enables them to expand their gape and swallow their prey whole. Their tongue allows them to sample air chemically and 'taste' their surroundings using a special sensory organ in the roof of the mouth known as Jacobson's organ. Some species of snake, especially vipers, also have pits around their lips that are filled with nerves especially sensitive to heat. Pit vipers use this feature as a heat sensor to search for small mammals in the dark.

Indian python: Sri Lanka's largest snake. (AS)

Forsten's cat snake (UH)

Perhaps the best known of snakes' adaptations is to be found in their teeth, which – in many species – have evolved grooves or hollows in the fashion of a hypodermic needle to deliver venom. The venom consists of specialised proteins which are either neurotoxic (affecting the nerve cells) or haemotoxic (affecting the blood cells). Some species have venom that exhibits both properties.

In Sri Lanka 95 species of snakes have been recorded in nine families. Little is known about the behaviour, ecology and distribution of many of them, and it is very likely that more species are yet to be discovered.

NON-VENOMOUS SNAKES

The island's largest snake is the Indian rock python (*Python molurus*), in the subfamily Pythonidae, which may exceptionally reach over 6m in length. This is a constrictor that kills its prey by asphyxiation, using sharp teeth to get a grip before wrapping its coils around its victim. The visitor's best chance of seeing a python is in one of the national parks such as Yala. However, pythons are still found on the outskirts of Colombo in the Talangama Wetland. The sand boa (*Gongylophis conica*) is a closely related species in another sub-family, the Boidae, but seldom exceeds 60cm in length. It is found in arid habitats from the southeast along to the drier parts of the North Central Province. During the day it sleeps in a burrow, emerging at night to hunt small mammals.

The blind snakes in the family Typhloidae live underground, where they feed on invertebrates such as worms, insects and spiders. These snakes are rarely seen unless rain forces them to the surface. Of the few species recorded in Sri Lanka, the majority are endemic. The brahminy blind snake (*Ramphotyphlops braminus*) is a small, worm-like dark snake under 20 cm long. It is probably the most familiar of the blind snakes as it may enter houses through pipes and drains in search of worms and insects. It has spread around the world through being transported in flower pots. It is parthenogenetic: all individuals are female and they can produce eggs without mating.

The family Colubridae comprises the most species. Although colubrids are known as 'typical snakes', they come in a wide variety of forms, including many that do not quite conform to this description. The rat snake (*Ptyas mucosa*) is probably the

most common snake in Sri Lanka. It is fast moving and appears superficially similar to the unrelated and venomous Indian cobra (*Naja naja*). This species can reach 3m, and is the second-largest snake on the island. It has round eyes, a bronze colour, and can be become used to people, who generally tolerate its presence. The widespread green vine snake (*Ahaetulla nasuta*) is a slender, beautiful snake with a pointed face. It is often encountered on trails through forests or suburban habitats, and relies on its green camouflage for concealment. The buff-striped keelback (*Amphiesma stolatum*) is another colubrid likely to be encountered on forest walks, especially near water. It grows to around 80cm in length, and has two pale buff stripes bordering its darker brown back.

Lucky visitors might see a snake gliding from one tree to another. Sri Lanka has two species of flying snake (genus *Chrysopela*). The ornate flying snake (*Chrysopela ornata*) has a body ringed in black and pale yellow, with a line of red spots, and grows to around 130cm. It frequents both forests and secondary vegetation and can enter houses in search of prey. The smaller Sri Lankan flying snake (*Chrysopela taprobanica*) is less colourful, being brown with dark rings, and is seen in the dry lowlands. Both species are active by day and can make spectacular glides between trees.

Locals believe the common vine snake strikes at the eyes. This is probably because its arboreal habits mean that it is often encountered at eye level. (GSW)

VENOMOUS SNAKES

Of the 95 species of snake recorded in Sri Lanka, only a few are venomous. Unfortunately some of these are amongst the most common, and often around human habitation, which provides a plentiful supply of rodents. Deaths due to snake bite in Sri Lanka average six per hundred thousand people. Although this figure is one of the highest in the world, it is nonetheless hardly reason to panic. Remember that snakes will always do their best to avoid you – which is why they are so seldom seen, despite their abundance. Over 95% of snakebites occur below the ankles, so a stout pair of shoes and long trousers can significantly reduce the risk. Simple precautions, such as not rummaging for firewood after dark, will also help.

Vipers (*Viperidae*) are generally solid, slow-moving snakes with a narrow neck and large, often triangular-shaped head. Their long fangs are located at the front of the mouth and folded back when not in use. The venom of the vipers is generally haemotoxic although the Sri Lankan race of the Russell's viper (*Daboia russelii*) has both haemotoxic and neurotoxic properties. This large, beautifully patterned species is responsible for almost half Sri Lanka's snakebite fatalities. It is normally active at dawn and dusk, but can be seen even during the hottest afternoon. Like many members of the viper family it is often slow to move, trusting on its camouflage to escape detection, but will strike extremely fast in self-defence. The much smaller and less venomous hump-nosed viper (*Hypnale hypnale*) is believed to be responsible for the greatest number of snakebites in Sri Lanka, although most adult victims survive. The saw-scaled viper (*Echis carinatus*) is confined to the arid areas, mainly in the north. It has a reputation for being aggressive and quick to bite, with untreated bites leading to serious complications, especially with the kidneys. When threatened, it can rub its coils together to make a rasping noise with its scales.

The green pit viper conceals itself in trees and hunts by stealth. (UH)

Indian cobra (Christopher Silva/Studio Times)

Cobras, kraits and coral snakes belong to the family Elapidae. They are generally alert, fast-moving snakes, and all carry neurotoxic venom. The Indian cobra is a common species with a potentially fatal bite. It has short fixed fangs and, when aroused, rears and erects a hood. Cobras are usually docile and quick to retreat from danger. They feed mainly on rats and mice. The kraits, however, feed on other snakes. The common krait (*Bungarus caeruleus*) is highly venomous, with bites leading to respiratory failure. It can be found in a variety of habitats and has been seen on footpaths near human habitation. During the day it is docile and likely to hide, but at night, bites are not uncommon. It is a dark snake with indistinct whitish rings. The Sri Lankan krait (*Bungarus ceylonicus*) is another highly venomous snake, with distinctive black and white banding. It is found mainly in the wet zone and is endemic to the island.

Sea snakes are highly aquatic, venomous snakes. Some give birth to live young and never come ashore, while sea kraits may bask on sand spits and islands and come ashore to lay eggs. Despite being highly venomous, sea snakes are not aggressive and serious bites are rare. They are easily identified by their tails, which are paddle-shaped as an adaptation for swimming. One of the most frequently encountered species is the hook-nosed sea snake (*Enhydrina schistosus*), which is dull black above. It is found from the Persian Gulf to Australia, and occurs in Sri Lanka in mangroves. The pelagic sea snake (*Pelamis platura*) is a widespread snake of the open ocean as well as the coasts. It grows up to 100cm long and is jet black above, with a sharply demarcated pale underside. The large yellow sea snake (*Hydrophis spiralis*) reaches 270cm long and has been recorded on the west coast.

Russell's viper has the longest fangs of any Sri Lankan snake. (GSW)

SNAKE BITES

Most snake bites are not fatal, simply because most species of snakes in Sri Lanka are not fatally venomous. Even bites from a venomous species may inject no venom (these being known as 'dry bites'). However, in the event of a bite from a venomous snake, treatment is essential. A victim does not die instantaneously from envenomation and prompt action can save a life. Many hospitals in Sri Lanka stock anti-venom serum for treating snake bites and one will usually be within easy reach along any serviceable road. Keep the victim calm and reassured and take him or her to the nearest hospital. Don't apply a tourniquet or make cuts around the bite, which will only increase the risk of infection. Immobilising the bitten limb will help slow the spread of venom. Try to make an accurate description of the snake, or kill it without further risk to yourself and take it with you for identification at the hospital.

Bites from vipers and cobras are painful, whereas krait bites are not. Haemotoxic bites cause internal bleeding whereas neurotoxic bites interfere with the transmission of nerve signals and can cause paralysis. Both lead to failure of the body's internal organs. The anti-venom used in Sri Lanka is a polyvalent type made from the venom of the cobra, common krait, Russell's viper and saw-scaled viper. As there are subtle differences in the venom of the subspecies found in Sri Lanka as opposed to those on mainland Asia, research is under way to develop a more effective local anti-venom.

CROCODILES

The order Crocodylia is one of four orders in the class Reptilia and embraces 21 species around the world. Two of these are found in Sri Lanka, both belonging to the family Crocodylidae: the marsh crocodile (*Crocodylus palustris*), also known as the mugger, and the saltwater crocodile (*Crocodylus porosus*), also known as the estuarine crocodile.

Crocodiles are primitive animals, whose basic form has remained unchanged for millions of years and features many adaptations for their aquatic, predatory lifestyle. Their mouth, perhaps surprisingly, is not watertight. However, they have a valve in the throat that shuts when they are underwater. The air duct from the nostrils opens below this valve, enabling them to breathe whilst floating with just nostrils and eyes above the water. The jaw muscles that open the mouth are quite weak – it is possible to hold a crocodile's mouth shut quite easily. This gives little cause for complacency, however, since the muscles that shut the jaws are so strong that prising them open is almost impossible.

The estuarine crocodile is the largest of the crocodilians and arguably the biggest reptile in the world. Large individuals may exceptionally measure over 6m in length and weigh more than one tonne. As the name suggest, this species is found in estuarine or brackish habitats close to river mouths. The Muthurajawela Wetland near Colombo is a good site, but visitors will need to take a boat ride at night to see them. A site for day-time viewing is Bundala National Park.

The marsh crocodile seldom grows much more than 4m in length, but an adult is nevertheless a fearsome beast. It can be distinguished from estuarine crocodiles by its less triangular face and snout, and also by lacking the pair of ridges that run from the eyes to the snout on the larger species. If left alone, the marsh crocodile overcomes its shyness of people. When the Vil Uyana Hotel at Sigiriya was built

The marsh crocodile is seldom a threat to people. But all crocodiles are best treated with caution.
(Studio Times)

around a manmade wetland, a couple of small marsh crocodiles quickly arrived and took up residence. Much to the concern of the manager, they also showed a keen interest in sharing the swimming pool.

Both species of crocodiles take a variety of animals. Fish and amphibians are an important source of food, and larger adults will prey on any large mammal they can seize from the water's edge. Livestock such as cattle and goats are sometimes taken, which may be one reason why crocodiles are persecuted. Today both species are much reduced in number – another reason for persecution being their meat, which is sometimes passed off as shark meat. The destruction of suitable nesting habitat and the spread of the water monitor, which feeds on crocodile eggs, also both play a

part. Some sources now estimate that no more than 300 estuarine crocodiles remain across the whole island. Although the marsh crocodile has a wider distribution, especially on inland lakes, fewer than 1,200 may be left.

Almost all accounts of man-eating by crocodiles can be attributed to the estuarine species – though this danger is rapidly disappearing with the crocodiles themselves. It is not uncommon to see

Baby crocodiles have many predators. (UH)

people bathing in lakes just a few metres away from large crocodiles, but these will be the far less dangerous marsh crocodiles. As a teenager I was birdwatching in a swamp when I attempted to step on an algae-encrusted log. The surprised log slipped into the water and fortunately my first brush with a saltwater crocodile did not bring a premature end to my natural history career.

Green turtle (*Chelonia midas*) (M Ushioda/WaterFrame)

TURTLES, TERRAPINS AND TORTOISES

The chelonians, comprising the sea turtles, freshwater turtles, terrapins and tortoises, make up another of the five orders in the class Reptilia. Five families are represented on the island: sea turtles (Cheloniidae and the Dermochelidae); Asian pond turtles (Bataguridae); soft-shelled turtles (Trionychidae); and the star tortoise (Testudinae). Most chelonians have a bony shell covered with horny shields or laminae – typically 13 on the upper shell, or carapace, and 12 on the under shell, or plastron. The number and relative positioning of these shields are unique to each species. The only turtles without bony shells are the soft-shelled turtles and the leatherback turtle (the sole member of the family Dermochelidae), both of which have leathery skin overlaying the carapace.

TERRAPINS

Terrapin is a name loosely applied to various species of freshwater turtle. The hard-shelled terrapin, also known as the spotted black turtle (*Melanochelys trijuga*), is one of the most common turtles in Sri Lanka. It is found throughout the island up to the highlands in ponds and streams, and occasionally appears in gardens in Colombo. At night it often forages on land for plants. The flapshell turtle (*Lissemys punctata*) is another common and widespread freshwater species. It has an omnivorous diet that includes other aquatic animals and carrion, and can be recognised by its distinctive raised nostrils.

TORTOISES

Tortoises are largely herbivorous, although they will scavenge on carrion, and are well known for their slow movement and longevity. Sri Lanka has just one species, the star tortoise (*Geochelone elegans*), whose domed carapace and plastron both bear a striking star-shaped pattern. This species is found throughout the dry lowlands, but its numbers have been greatly reduced by collection for the pet trade. It is also vulnerable to the seasonal fires that are started for slash and burn (*chena*) agriculture.

Collection as a pet and for its shell has had an adverse impact on the star tortoise. (GSW)

SEA TURTLES

Sea turtles differ in several respects from other chelonians. Unlike most turtles, they cannot withdraw their heads and legs inside their shell at the first hint of danger. However, their manoeuvrability in the water and strong bite help them to fend off predators. Like all turtles, they breathe air. However, special vascular organs near the throat and vent allow them to utilise dissolved oxygen so they can rest or sleep underwater for several hours (although during normal activity they will surface every five minutes or so). Thousands of sea turtles perish in fishing nets each year.

Sea turtles mate out at sea and females can store sperm for a few years. They come ashore at night to lay their eggs, showing an uncanny ability to navigate hundreds of kilometres to the beach where they were born. Quite often a female excavates one burrow and then moves onto a second before laying. This may be an anti-predation strategy. Each clutch may consist of up to 200 golf-ball-sized eggs. Some species may lay several clutches at intervals of around two weeks. The sex of the hatchlings is determined by incubation temperature. After hatching, they may take two days to emerge, which usually happens under cover of darkness, whereupon they head staight down the beach back towards the sea. Strong lights on shore may disorient them during this journey. It is estimated that less than one-hundreth of one percent of all hatchlings survives to adulthood. Wild pigs dig out the nests even before the eggs hatch, while terrestrial predators, including birds, crabs, dogs,

The loggerhead turtle is one of the rarest turtles to nest in Sri Lanka. (G Nowak/WaterFrame)

NESTING SEA TURTLES IN SRI LANKA

Different species of sea turtle come ashore to lay their eggs at different times of year
Visitors should approach a nesting sea turtle only after it has begun to lay eggs. Even
then, you should avoid using torchlights.

Species	Nesting periods	Sites
Leatherback	May–June; October–December	Induruwa, Kosgoda, Rekawa
Loggerhead	September–March	Kosgoda, Rekawa
Green	January–March	Induruwa, Kosgoda, Rekawa
Hawksbill	December–January; April–June	Bentota, Kosgoda
Olive ridley	September–January	Induruwa, Kosgoda, Rekawa, Bentota

Loggerhead turtle hatchling
(M Ushioda/WaterFrame)

mongooses and jackals, pick off the hatchlings before they reach the waves. In the
sea, sharks and other predatory fish are waiting for them.

Five species of sea turtle come ashore in Sri Lanka. The leatherback turtle
(*Dermochelys coriacea*) is the largest, with adults weighing up to one tonne. Its diet
consists mainly of jellyfish, and sadly many die when they mistake discarded plastic
bags for this food. The olive ridley turtle (*Lepidochelys olivacea*) is the smallest. It nests
in a number of sites on the west and south coasts, including off the highly developed
coasts around Colombo, Dehiwela and Mount Lavinia, and in some places (but not
in Sri Lanka) gathers in tens of thousands to take part in mass nestings, called
arribadas. The hawksbill turtle (*Eretmochelys imbricata*) feeds almost exclusively on
sponges and is threatened by the illegal trade in 'tortoiseshell' jewellery. The green
turtle (*Chelonia mydas*) actually has an olive or brown carapace, and derives its name
from the colour of its fat. This species is found around sandy coasts, and people
snorkelling off Unawatuna and Hikkaduwa regularly report sightings. The
loggerhead turtle (*Retmochelys imbricata*) is the rarest Sri Lankan species. It has a
reddish-brown carapace, and strong jaws with which to crush the shells of the
crustaceans and molluscs on which it feeds.

Jerdon's bullfrog is the largest amphibian on the island. (GSW)

AMPHIBIANS

Amphibians are an ancient order of animals, the oldest of the vertebrate animals to have adapted to an existence on land. Unlike reptiles, their skin does not have a covering of scales but is a moist membrane that is also used for respiration. All amphibians take in oxygen and release carbon dioxide through their skin. The skin has to be moist for this exchange of gases to take place, which is why amphibians are largely restricted to damp habitats.

The eggs of amphibans are not covered in a shell but in a porous membrane. In some frogs, the larval stage develops inside the egg. But in most species a larval stage, or tadpole, hatches and needs water to complete its metamorphosis into adulthood. This intermediate stage in the development from egg to adult is another factor that separates amphibians from reptiles.

Two orders of amphibian occur in Sri Lanka. The Gymnophiona are the caecilians, of which Sri Lanka has four species. These limbless creatures, with their concealed eyes and ring-like folds of skin, resemble earthworms. They lay their eggs in mud or water and the larvae live in water. Adults live in moist places on land, such as under logs and leaf litter. At any sign of danger they quickly burrow into the ground.

The second order of amphibians, the Anura, comprises the frogs and toads. Sri Lanka has more than its fair share, including, among others, eight species of toad (Bufonidae), ten species of narrow-mouthed tree frog (Microhylidae) and 66 species of old world tree frog (Ranidae). The number of species will continue to rise: at the time of writing, more than 50 are in the process of being described to science.

Toads are easily identifed by their warty skin and squat proportions. The common toad (*Bufo melanostictus*) is one species most likely to be seen by visitors, as it is widespread and found in a range of habitats from forests to gardens. In lowland

Above The common hourglass frog
(*Polypedates cruciger*) (UH)
Right The mountain hourglass frog
(*Polypedates eques*) (UH)

Left The anthropogenic shrub frog
(*Philautus hoipolloi*) (PA)
Below The leaf-nesting shrub frog
(*Philautus femoralis*) (WHT)

Long-snouted tree frog (Polypedates longinasus) is found in the under-storey of rainforests up to 1,300m. (UH)

wet zone forests, Kotagama's toad (*Bufo kotagami*) is easily mistaken for the common toad. A colourful species that sometimes turns up in gardens is the Sri Lanka bullfrog (*Microhyla taprobanica*). A pair of bright red markings and a rotund body shape help to identify it. Another familiar species is the Indian green frog (*Euphlyctis hexadactylus*). An adult of this species seems the archetypal frog of fairy tales. Anyone hoping to kiss one to turn it into a prince should also stroke its throat: if the throat is warty, it is an Indian green frog; if the throat is smooth, it is probably the slightly smaller but very similar-looking Indian skipper frog (*Euphlyctis cyanophlyctis*).

The subfamily Rhacophirinae contains many shrub frogs. These include the pale blue Asanka's shrub frog (*Philautus asankai*), found in the mid hills, and the spotted tree frog (*Polypedates maculatus*), which enjoys a wide distribution in both dry and wet zones and may often be found sharing a visitor's bathroom. By contrast, the long-snouted tree frog (*Polypedates longinasus*) is restricted to lowland wet zone forests. The wide variety of shrub frogs means there is hardly a damp habitat in Sri Lanka that is not occupied by one or more species. At night, these frogs maintain a cacophony of clicks, tinkles and barks.

A number of frogs in the genus *Philautus* give birth through direct development after laying their eggs, obviating the tadpole stage. This is believed to make them less vulnerable to dry periods. In Sri Lanka, the diversity of species in this genus, with perhaps a hundred new to science, makes it one of the most important species radiations to be discovered anywhere over the last century or so.

The presence of amphibians and their levels of diversity are good indicators of the health of the environment. A decline in amphibians has been observed worldwide. A number of reasons have been suggested: increased levels of UV radiation as a result of the thinning ozone layer; deteriorating water quality due to the run-off of agricultural chemicals; untreated household and industrial waste in waterways; the use of toxic sprays on farmlands; and the outright destruction of habitat. In Sri Lanka some species have vanished forever and are now known only from museum specimens, while the distribution of others has been severely reduced or fragmented. Das's dwarf toad (*Adenomus dasi*), for instance, is now known only from a few unpolluted streams in the highlands near Moray Estate in the Peak Wilderness, though it was once widespread across the island. As rainforest is cleared for tea and other commercial crops, it is possible that some species will vanish before science even finds them.

INVERTEBRATES

Red damselfly (DM)

Invertebrates are animals without backbones – or, to the uninformed, simply 'bugs'. This umbrella term covers everything from worms and snails to spiders and insects, and makes up by far the largest proportion of animal species on earth, about 1.8 million species in total. Compare this with the 50,000 species of vertebrate animals. Most invertebrates are too small to grab our attention and, even with more visible groups, identification may be impossible for all but the scientist. Scientists estimate that as little as 4% of all invertebrate species have been described to science. To guide the newcomer, this book describes briefly a few of the more conspicuous groups, including those that the visitor is most likely to encounter.

LOWER INVERTEBRATES
LEECHES
Leeches, like earthworms, belong to the phylum Annelida, which comprises around 7,000 species worldwide. Some are terrestrial; others are aquatic. Most visitors would rather avoid all of them. This is because leeches feed mainly on the blood of mammals. Their body is effectively one big stomach, with suckers at both ends and sharp mouthparts that latch onto their prey.

Leeches are absent from high elevations and dry areas, but a walk in a lowland rainforest is bound to attract them. They concentrate along footpaths and game trails with a regular traffic of people and other animals. A leech can survive for more than a month on a full meal of blood, so a relatively low number of prey animals can sustain a large number of leeches. Wearing a 'leech sock' made of raw cotton over your usual socks is an effective deterrent. But pulling them off can leave part of their mouthparts embedded, which can result in an unpleasant wound that lasts for days.

Acavus land snails
(GSW)

LAND SNAILS
In recent years land snails have gained a new focus, thanks to the work of scientists from the British Museum of Natural History working with Sri Lankan scientists under a Darwin Initiative research project. The land snails of Sri Lanka are special for a number of reasons, including their high rate of endemism: over 90% of species being unique to the island. They share an evolutionary lineage with the land snails of Madagascar, from when the two landmasses were joined in the supercontinent of Gondwanaland. By studying these snails, scientists have learned much about the rate of evolutionary processes. They can even deduce the composition of the earth's atmosphere in its geological past by studying the ratio of certain carbon and oxygen isotopes in preserved snail shells.

Many of the larger and prominent land snails that visitors see clinging to tree trunks are in the genus *Acavus*. Some villagers drink the protein-rich, mucous secretion that accumulates around them, but unaccustomed visitors may be better off sticking to the energy drinks on sale in the local supermarket.

ARTHROPODS

The arthropods (Arthropoda) are a diverse group characterised by jointed limbs, an external skeleton (called an exoskeleton) and compound eyes. Anyone who has a local prawn curry will soon be familiar with the basics of arthropod structure. There are six main classes: the Crustacea include the shrimps, crabs and lobsters encountered at the dining table (though do also keep a lookout for the freshwater crabs in the island's streams and rivers, of which 51 species described to date are endemic to the island); the Arachnida comprise the spiders, scorpions and ticks; the Myriapoda comprise the centipedes and millipedes; and most numerous of all are the myriad creatures that make up the class Insecta.

MILLIPEDES AND CENTIPEDES

Millipedes and centipedes (Myriapoda) are not too difficult to tell apart, as millipedes have rounded bodies and generally move at a leisurely pace, while centipedes are flatter bodied and wriggle along at speed. Both favour damp locations. Millipedes feed mostly on decaying plant matter and play a useful role in the recycling of nutrients. Some species of millipedes are diurnal, including one that reaches nearly 15cm in length and is common in lowland forests. Centipedes are carnivorous and hunt at night. They can inflict a painful bite. Both millipedes and centipedes have separate sexes and lay eggs.

Centipedes have one pair of legs per segment. Some species pack a painful bite. (PA)

Myrmarachne plataleoides. This spider belongs to the salticidae family or jumping spiders. (SB)

SPIDERS AND SCORPIONS

Spiders and scorpions are arachnids (Arachnida). They differ from insects by having eight legs, no antennae and a body divided into two, not three, principal sections. They also have a pair of appendages called pedipalps, arm-like limbs used for seizing prey, and a pair of fang-like chelicerae at the front. Both spiders and scorpions are carnivorous, preying mostly on other arthropods.

Scorpions carry a sting in their tail, which they use to immobilise prey whilst seizing it in their pincer-like pedipalps. Males perform an elaborate mating ritual, 'dancing' around the female to manoeuvre a sperm package deposited on the ground into her genital opening. The young hatch alive inside the female's body and ride on her for a week or so.

In spiders the pedipalps are not modified into weapons, as in scorpions. Instead, the males use them as a tactile organ for transferring sperm to the female. The chelicerae are modified for immobilising prey by injecting poison. But perhaps the spiders' most fascinating adaptation is their ability to use silk, spinning it from four special spinnerets at the tip of their abdomen. They use this to cast a web in which to trap prey. Sometimes they will also wrap prey in silk until they are ready to eat it. Relative to their diameter, these silk strands are as strong as steel.

To date, 501 species of spider have been described from Sri Lanka, though the true number may be much higher. The most prominent are the *Nephila* species or giant wood spiders. The large ones are the females; the tiny ones at the edge of the web are the males. Mating is a particularly fraught experience for male spiders, since they may end up as food for the female. Some species strum on the web to put the female in a receptive mood. Others aim to appease her with a gift of a tasty morsel.

Giant wood spider (Devaka Seneviratne/Studio Times)

Other spiders include the Araneidae (true orb weavers) and Tetragnatidae (long-jawed spiders), which weave beautiful small webs. The Gasteracantha spiders are notable for the 'shell' on their bodies, which tapers into a sharp point on either side. The jumping spiders (Salticidae) do not use webs for catching prey, but pounce on it instead. *Myrmarchne plataleoides* is one of several species that mimics ants in order to deter their enemies. Certain crab spiders do the same thing, but with the more insidious motive of preying on the ants.

INSECTS

Insects (Insecta) are distinguished from other arthropods by having a three-segmented body (consisting of head, thorax and abdomen) and three pairs of jointed legs. They are the most abundant life form on Earth, with probably over a million species worldwide. In Sri Lanka, a survey of described insects done in 2003 found 11,144 species, which made up over half the known organisms in Sri Lanka and 81% of the known animals.

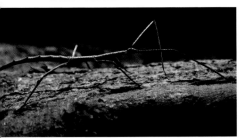

Top In some stick insects only females are known. (Studio Times)

Above Leaf insects are perfectly camouflaged in their natural environment. (Studio Times)

It is not possible in a book of this kind to tackle all the orders of insects. I have thus focused on two popular and conspicuous groups: butterflies, part of the Lepidoptera (which also include the more numerous but harder-to-identify moths); and dragonflies and damselflies, which make up the Odonata. But some other orders first deserve a brief mention, too.

The order Phasmida includes the intriguing praying mantises and stick insects. Most have extraordinary camouflage which, in stick insects, enables them to hide from predators and, in praying mantises, enables them to ambush prey. Many species of stick insect are parthenogenic, the females laying eggs without fertilisation by a male. In fact in many species, no males are known.

The order Neuroptera contains the graceful lacewings and the antlions, which, with their long translucent wings, bear a superficial resemblance to some damselflies. Antlions are best known for the larval stage of some species, in which the larvae create a sandy, saucer-like pit and lie buried at the centre with just their mouthparts protruding. Passing insects slip into the pit and are sucked dry by the larva.

The large carpenter bees are often mistaken for beetles. (RK)

The beetles and weevils are in the Coleoptera. With over 400,000 species worldwide, this is the most prolific of the insect orders, and 3,033 species have so far been described in Sri Lanka. The shell of coleopterans is formed by the forewings hardened into a protective cover known as an elytra. In the dry lowlands, watch out for dung beetles rolling a ball of dung away with their hind feet. They play a vital role important in ensuring that the landscape does not get buried in the dung of herbivorous animals.

The order Hymenoptera contains social insects such as ants, bees and wasps. Bees play a very imporatnt role as a pollinator of plants. Communal species have a complex social structure, with a queen bee founding a colony that is maintained by workers and soldiers. Solitary species include carpenter bees – large, black insects that drill into wood to lay their eggs. Wasps are distinguished from bees by their thin 'waist'. Some species lay their eggs in the larvae of other insects, the young hatching and eating their host alive. The first species of wasp known to provide pollen to its young, *Krombeinictus nordenae*, was discovered in Sri Lanka.

The social complexity of ants is just as amazing as that of bees and wasps. No fewer than 181 species have so far been described from Sri Lanka. Some 'milk' other insects, such as aphids or certain caterpillars, for their sweet secretions of honeydew. Many have a special relationship with plants: the ants provide the plant with protection and the plants exude a sweet sap as a reward. A common ant in towns and villages is the red weaver ant (*Oecophylla smaragdina*), known locally as a *dimiya*. This species weaves leaves together with a sticky thread and lays its eggs inside. Trees can become festooned with its nests.

Flies are in the order Diptera, which contains several unwelcome species. The house fly (*Musca domestica*) is a vector for many diseases, including typhoid and cholera. Even less welcome are mosquitoes, of which Sri Lanka has nearly

The presence of termite mounds shows that soil is being turned over and organic matter recycled. They also make convenient resting places for a variety of reptiles, including this rat snake. (Studio Times)

200 species. The adults generally feed on plant juices, but females also take blood. Malaria, which is responsible for a million deaths annually worldwide, is spread by *Anopheles* mosquitos, which transfer *Plasmodium* parasites to people. In Sri Lanka the anti-malarial campaigns have been succesful. Chikungunya and dengue fever, however, are spread by *Aedes* mosquitos and have recently become more of a public health concern.

The dry lowlands are dotted with termite mounds. There are 69 species of termite, in the order Isoptera, so far recorded from Sri Lanka, of which 41 are endemic. These social insects are organised along similar lines to social bees: each colony has a female founder, and thousands of workers and soldiers. Using pheromones to communicate with each other, many species (though not all) create a huge mound. A series of chambers inside performs many different functions, including incubation and ventilation. The eggs will only incubate successfully if the temperature is kept within a certain band. Some termites can be extremely destructive by feeding on wood, which they digest using special bacteria to break down the cellulose. But other species live in forest habitats and cause no problems for people. Termites everywhere play a pivotal role in maintaining the health of ecosystems by recycling carbon and nitrogen, and enriching soils.

BUTTERFLIES

Butterflies and moths are winged insects that belong to the order Lepidoptera. There are no absolute differences between the two, but some general rules of thumb are helpful: butterflies generally fly by day, whereas most moths fly by night; butterflies are generally more brightly coloured; the antennae of butterflies have a club tip, whereas those of moths are generally feathery or thick; and most moths have a coupling mechanism that links the fore and hind wings in flight, which is absent in all butterflies but one.

Sri Lanka has 243 species of butterfly, of which the casual visitor will encounter a good number. Among the more notable is the blue oakleaf (*Kallima philarchus*). This is one of many whose beautiful colours are concealed when it settles, revealing only the camouflage pattern of the underwings, which exactly mimics a dead leaf. Another to use this trick is the white orange tip (*Ixias marianne*). Mud sips are good places to observe butterflies, allowing a chance to see rare species such as the five-bar swordtail (*Pathysa antiphates*), which may join more abundant species like common bluebottles (*Graphium sarpedon*). Mud sipping is when butterflies perch on the ground to sip dissolved nutrients or minerals in the soil. After the rains, in parks like Yala or Wilpattu, you may encounter hundreds, mainly whites and yellows in the family Pieridae, clustered around the puddles on the jeep tracks.

BUTTERFLIES OF THE GARDEN

One of the most striking garden butterflies is the common jezebel (*Delias eucharis*). Its hind wings are mainly yellow, edged with a series of red cones. This species likes

The dark blue tiger is distasteful to predators, thanks to alkaloids absorbed during its larval stage. (GSW)

The beautiful crimson rose is widespread in the lowlands. (GSW)

to fly at treetop level, by contrast with the nearly all-white psyche, which flutters close to the ground. Grass yellows are hard to tell apart, but the common grass yellow (*Eurema hecabe*) is a frequent visitor to weeds. The striking tawny coster (*Acraea violae*), an orange butterfly with bold black patterning, can also show up in gardens. It is the only member of its family – the Acraeidae – found in Sri Lanka.

Jak trees attract barons (*Euthalia aconthea*), which are not as regal as the name might suggest, while citrus trees attract the swift-flying lime butterfly (*Papilio demoleus*), one of several species in the Swallowtail family (Papilionidae) to visit gardens. The widespread crimson rose (*Pachliopta hector*), with its bright crimson body, is also often seen in gardens. The blues are never easy to identify, though a palm tree may host the plains cupid (*Chilades pandava*), also known as the cycad blue. These butterflies are very territorial and swirling aerial duels often take place. The common palmfly (*Elymnias hypermnestra*) is another butterfly attracted to palm trees. Palmflies have a curious habit of running along a leaf when they land, as though rolling on rollers.

The tailed jay is an active insect with a frantic flight, seldom seen basking like this. (GSW)

BUTTERFLIES OF THE FOREST

If I had to name my favourite forest butterfly it would be the tree nymph (*Idea iasonia*). These black-and-white butterflies float delicately in the wind like fairies, and whenever I enter Sinharaja Rainforest, a few seem to keep me company along the path. The plum judy (*Abisara echerius*) is a butterfly of the dark understorey, though at some times of year it seems to prefer the sunlit edge of footpaths, its dark wings showing a beautiful iridescent violet when the light catches them. The clipper (*Parthenos sylvia*) is a large blue butterfly that flies with a hump-backed appearance. Adopting a similar technique is the smaller but more energetic commander (*Moduza procris*); at rest a broad white band on the upperwing makes this species easy to identify.

The common Indian crow is one of several similar looking butterflies. (RK)

The bamboo forests hold a few rare species that are confined to this remnant habitat. These include the Southern duffer (*Discophora lepida*) and the Cingalese bushbrown (*Mycalesis rama*). Sinharaja, Morapitiya and Bodhingala are good sites for these rarities. These forests also hold other colourful butterflies such as the cruiser (*Vindula erota*), common birdwing (*Troides darsius*) and the blue mormon (*Papilio polymnestor*). The last two are the largest butterflies in Sri Lanka.

The blue mormon is one of Sri Lanka's two largest butterfly species. (GSW)

The scarlet basker has dark basal area to its hind-wings, which helps to identify it. (GSW)

DRAGONFLIES AND DAMSELFLIES

The Ordonata, loosely known as dragonflies, comprise one of the smaller and more ancient orders of insect, with fossil records dating back to the Permian period, 230–280 million years ago. Dragonflies (Anisoptera) can be distinguished from damselflies (Zygoptera) by their 'chunkier' build and their habit of perching with wings spread open. Damselflies are usually slimmer and more fragile-looking, with eyes that do not meet over the forehead, and hold their wings closed over the body.

Of the 118 species of Ordonata that have been recorded on Sri Lanka, an astonishing 52 are endemic. This makes them very important to the study of the island's biodiversity. Nonetheless, relatively little is known about them. The elusive adjutant (*Aethrimanta brevipennis*) had not been recorded for over 100 years until I photographed one at the Hunas Falls Hotel and the scientist Matjaz Bedjanic identified it. Now it is turning up everywhere! Another dragonfly scientist, Karen Conniff, has also been uncovering a great many rarities, some not far from Colombo. Thanks to people like Matjaz and Karen, a number of Sri Lankans are discovering a new area of interest and our knowledge is steadily increasing.

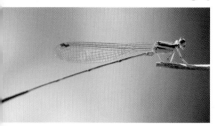

The two-spotted threadtail is found along forested streams. (GSW)

108

DRAGONFLIES OF TOWN AND GARDEN

Dragonflies may turn up in a variety of domestic and urban environments,though they invariably need water in which to lay their eggs. Wanderers are freshly matured adults that have travelled from their hatching sites, following an instinct to disperse that keeps the gene pool fluid. Those that find a pond or suitable drain with unpolluted fresh water may succeed in breeding.

The yellow waxtail (*Ceriagrion coromandelianum*) and painted waxtail (*Ceriagrion cerinorubellum*) are two common urban damselflies. The male yellow waxtail is easy to identify with its uniform yellow colour, the female being duller and green. The painted waxtail is a two-tone creature in green and red, with both sexes being similar. Despite this bright colouration, it is easily overlooked because of its unobtrusive habits. The diminutive wandering wisp (*Agriocnemis pygmaea*) is just a few centimetres in length, and is easily lost to sight as it weaves around low-lying vegetation.

Colombo's gardens attract a variety of dragonflies from its extensive surrounding marshlands. The marsh dancer (*Onychargia atrocyana*) usually perches in pairs in bushes at about waist height. The variable flutterer (*Rhyothemis variegata*), with its gold-spangled wings, seems to thrive on even the most polluted waterways. The equally striking pied parasol (*Neurothemis tullia*) is probably one of the most abundant dragonflies in Sri Lanka, turning up everywhere from gardens to paddy fields.

DRAGONFLIES OF THE FOREST

The forested streams of sites such as Bodhinagala, Sinharaja and Morapitiya are rich in endemic dragonflies. Some species are hard to tell apart in the field and others may be overlooked entirely. But most visitors should be able to recognise a few. These include the dark forestwraith (*Platysticta apicalis*), a dragonfly with dark

The wandering wisp is a small damselfly that keeps very low. (RK)

Adam's gem is found along fast flowing streams or unpolluted ditches. (GSW)

wingtips to and a jet black 'saddle' on its thorax; Wall's grappletail (*Heliogomphus walli*), which perches on broad-leaved plants besides jungle tracks; and the Sri Lanka cascader (*Zygonyx iris*), a large, dark dragonfly that often perches up high beside streams. No stream is complete without a few shining gossamerwings (*Euphaea splendens*) perched on the rocks. These look black when perched, but become a shimmering emerald in flight.

The former logging track of Sinharaja may reveal a mysterious dragonfly, Frustohfer's junglewatcher (*Hylaeothemis fruhstorferi*), which is known reliably only from this site. It is black with white stripes. The black-tipped flashwing (*Vestalis apicalis*) is a spectacular shiny green damselfly that also occasionally turns up beside the logging tracks, but more often near streams. The marsh skimmer (*Orthetrum luzonicum*), with its beautiful blue abdomen in the male, prefers higher elevations. The pink skimmer (*Orthetrum pruinosum*) is widespread in wetlands, from open marshes to small forest ponds. The dark head distinguishes it from the widespread oriental scarlet (*Crocothemis servilia*), which is a striking scarlet all over, except for the translucent wings.

The mountain reedling (*Indolestes gracilis*) is not uncommon in reed-fringed highland ponds and looks superficially similar to lowland species such as the scalloped spreadwing (*Lestes praemorsus*). The introduction of predatory trout to the highland streams during the 19th century for game fishing may have resulted in the extinction of montane dragonfly species. In which case, we will never know how many we have lost.

THE
UNDERWATER WORLD

Coral grouper (RD)

Some scientists estimate that more species of animals exist underwater than on terra firma. This is hardly surprising, given that more than 70% of the earth's surface is covered in water. Besides, it was relatively late in evolutionary history that animals colonised the land. Aquatic animals have been around for very much longer and have had more time to evolve into a multitude of species. Many land animals are evolved from animals with an aquatic lineage. In a few cases, the reverse holds true. For example, the whales and dolphins are descdended from terrestrial ancestors.

Many aquatic animals are microscopic. But even among the visible species, there are too many for the scope of a general wildlife guide. Coverage here is thus restricted to freshwater fish and the more obvious forms of marine life a casual visitor is likely to encounter.

FRESHWATER FISH

Sri Lanka has 88 native species of freshwater fish, of which 44 are endemic. This does not include those found in the island's many manmade lakes, which were introduced from Africa. Sri Lanka has no indigenous lake fish, so native species found in lakes are those adapted to rivers that have entered lakes by accident – either due to dispersal of their eggs by animals or because floods have carried them from one body of water to another.

A freshwater stream or river in a rainforest like Sinharaja or Kanneliya allows an opportunity to observe the stratification of different guilds of species. Bottom dwellers such as common spiny loach (*Lepidocephalichthys thermalis*), banded mountain loach (*Schistura notostigma*) and stonesucker (*Garra ceylonensis*) are usually solitary and territorial. Stonesuckers have a suction disc for attaching themselves to the bottom of the oxygen-rich, fast-flowing streams in which they occur. Fish of the mid and upper levels usually swim in small groups. Midwater fish include the barbs (*Puntius* spp.) and the beautiful paradise combtail (*Belontia signata*). Danios and panchaxes occupy the upper waters, and their dorsal surfaces are relatively flat.

Black ruby barb (*Puntius nigrofasciatus*) is an endemic confined to forested streams. (UH)

Cumming's barb (UH)

Some of Sri Lanka's freshwater fish are familar to the aquarium trade. Species such as the black ruby barb (*Puntius nigrofasciatus*), cherry barb (*Puntius titteya*), Cuming's barb (*Puntius cumingii*) and golden rasbora (*Rasbora vaterifloris*) have been exported in huge numbers over decades. Paradoxically, others are still little known and many await description. Like its amphibians and other groups, many of Sri Lanka's fish species show 'point endemism', which means they occur in just one locality. The asoka barb (*Puntius asoka*) is one example, with just two populations being documented – both from the Kelani River basin.

Some fish have unusual reproduction strategies. In the ocellated pipefish (*Microphis ocellatus*), which frequents turbid water near the water's edge, males carry the eggs in a special groove on the underside of their bodies. In the combtail (*Belontia signata*), which can be observed in shaded, slow-flowing streams in protected forests such as Sinharaja, females lay their eggs in a nest of bubbles, which is then closely guarded by the male. The male can be so aggressive that it will not even tolerate females approaching the eggs.

The black-lined barb (*Puntius pleurotaeria*) is found in the southwestern hills. (UH)

The gobies are a complex group of fishes that are adapted to living in fast-flowing water. Some species are so small that they can be identified only under a microscope. Several are known to spend their larval stage at sea: the eggs wash down to the sea where the larvae emerge; later as adults, they swim back upriver.

Ghost crabs like the higher reaches of sandy beaches and can seem to disappear with their camouflage. (RD)

MARINE LIFE

The oceans teem with life, with a multitude of species still awaiting description. Sri Lanka, surrounded by sea, has a rich diversity of marine habitats, each with its own community of sea creatures. Some of these are described below. Although the oceans are vast and may seem infinite, we are now causing enough damage for its effects to be felt. We have, for instance, pushed many fish and marine mammals to the brink of extinction by over-fishing, and have poisoned foodwebs through the introduction of persistent organic pollutants (POPs). Global warming, however, may yet pose the greatest environmental threat of all.

ALONG THE SEASHORE

Sri Lanka has 1,700km of coastline, which provides a little-explored but extensive series of habitats, from sandy beaches to rock pools. The inter-tidal zone is home to a variety of invertebrates. These include annelids or segmented worms, some of which (the Errantia) swim freely, while others (the Sedentaria) live in tubes that they construct for shelter. Among the latter, some build burrows in the sand and use feathery tentacles to sweep in particles of food. Others, such as lugworms, ingest the mud around them and extract the organic content, leaving behind telltale mud casts.

Crabs are crustaceans, which, like insects, belong to the phylum Arthropoda – animals with jointed legs and a segmented body encased in an exoskeleton (see page 117). In fact, most marine arthropods are crustaceans. They form an important part of the food chain, and many are a major food source for people. Crabs, like lobsters and prawns, are decapods, with a pair of legs modified into claws and their eyes on stalks. They carry their eggs under the abdomen, and can regenerate lost or damaged limbs, which grow back after a few moults.

Ghost crabs (*Ocypode*) are intermediate between marine crabs and terrestrial crabs. They can go for long periods out of water and are abundant on the upper reaches of the tideline, where they scuttle at high speed along the sand. Fiddler crabs (*Uca*) are also semi-terrestrial, and live primarily in mangroves. Males have one claw significantly larger than the other, which they use to signal during their courtship display. The brine shrimp found in salt pans is an unusual animal: it swims on its back and is sometimes found in female-only colonies that do not need males for their propagation. Barnacles are crustaceans that look like snails (Gastropods) because of their tent-like shell. They have feathery legs that extend when submerged and work like a net to capture food.

Sri Lanka's beaches are littered with seashells. These are the remains of living animals that belong to the phylum Mollusca. Molluscs fall broadly into two classes: snails (Gastropoda) have spirally twisted shells; bivalves (Pelecypoda) have hinged shells that open into two halves. Limpets, which cling tenaciously to rocks, are gastropods, as are many of the showy shells that are often found on the beach, including cowries, whelks, periwinkles, horn-shells and the impressive Venus's comb (*Murex tribulus*). Most of these are carnivorous. Oysters, clams and scallops are all bivalves. The gills of an oyster are more than an apparatus for breathing: they also act as a filter for collecting microscopic food particles.

UNDER THE SEA

Sri Lanka's coral reefs are not as famous as those of the nearby Maldives. Some, such as the inshore reefs around Hikkaduwa, have been badly damaged by coral mining for the construction industry. Nevertheless there is a vast array of fish and other animals in those that remain intact, such as at Unawatuna. Certain reef species are found only off the coast of Sri Lanka, and new species of fish are still being discovered.

MARINE INVERTEBRATES

Among the most obvious highlights of any underwater dive are the coral formations. Although these look like plants, they are actually assemblages of animals called polyps, from the phylum Coelentara. They produce a poisonous fluid for capturing tiny prey items suspended in the water. Sea anemones, which are also colenterates, have a special symbiotic relationship with certain fish: the stinging tentacles of the anemones help shelter the fish from predators; the fish, in turn, aggressively defend their hosts from other browsing fish. Most colenterates attach themselves to a firm substrate, over time contributing to the development of the reef by excreting

Blue anemone (DJ)

Crown jellyfish (RD)

calcium carbonate that they ingest from the sea. Others are free living: a jellyfish is actually a community of different polyps, with each group having specialised functions. Some jellyfish, such as the Portuguese man-of-war (*Physalia*) have a sting powerful enough to harm a human. This is one of four stinging species of jellyfish found in Sri Lankan waters.

Another interesting association to be seen underwater exists between fish and cleaner shrimps (*Stenopus* spp.). The shrimps set up a 'cleaning station', where they wave their claws to attract fish. When fish arrive, they wait patiently while the cleaner shrimps clamber around them picking off skin parasites. A fish will not swallow cleaners, even if they enter its mouth. This relationship is beneficial to both parties: the shrimps get a meal and the fish get a clean. As a result Stenopus shrimps are regularly exported from Sri Lanka to aquarium enthusiasts around the world.

Hermit crabs (*Pagurus* spp.) are often found on the beach, dragging along the abandoned shell in which they have taken shelter. Sea anemones may also attach themselves to the shell, providing additional protection to the crab, which – in turn – provides transport to the anemone. Many species of crab habitually carry a piece of sponge, shell or even plant matter over their backs, as camouflage. Some have even evolved a pair of hooked legs arched over the back for this purpose.

Octopuses and cuttlefish belong to the class Cephalapoda. Like snails, they are molluscs, although you wouldn't guess this from their appearance. Octopuses are intelligent animals with a

Starfish prey mainly on bivalves, using their tube feet to force open their shells with vacuum suction. (RD)

number of interesting adaptations. They can change colour, and can squirt a jet of water to propel themselves through the water. They can also eject a black liquid to discolour the water around them as a kind of smokescreen. The head of the octopus is actually its body, a muscular sac containing its eyes and mouth.

The phylum Echinodermata is characterised by a five-sided symmetry, and includes animals such as starfish and brittle stars. In order to get around, these animals create a partial vacuum in their tube feet by pumping water in and out. They use this same vacuum to exert pressure on the bivalves on which they feed. Starfish enclose their prey with their stomachs in order to feed on them. Most have five limbs, but some may have four or six. If they lose one, they can grow another.

Brittle stars are superficially similar, but their limbs are much longer and slimmer, and are also many-jointed. Sea urchins (Ehinoidea) are very distinct, being protected by a mass of sharp quills that can inflict painful wounds. A dive to a good coral reef may also reveal feather stars (Crinoidea) and sea cucumbers (Holothuroidea). The former have ten arms, which they flap to swim. The latter can throw out their internal organs if disturbed; these soon grow back again.

REEF FISH

After the corals themselves, the most conspicuous reef animals are fish. Sri Lanka has over 1,000 species of marine fish. In rocky habitats, divers might encounter the two largest of the moray eels, the giant moray (*Gymnothorax javanicus*) and honeycomb moray (*Gymnothorax favogineus*). Despite their fearsome reputation, moray eels will generally leave divers alone. The same applies to the lionfish (*Pterois volitans*) and scorpionfish (*Scorpaenidae*), whose venomous spines are not to be stepped on.

The mangrove snapper or mangrove jack (*Lutjanus argentimaculatus*) spends the early part of its life in rivers and estuaries, where it is a popular sport fish. Adults move back to sea and out to progressively deeper water as they grow older. Goatfish (Mullidae) have sensitive fleshy appendages around their mouth, called barbels, which can detect prey buried under the sand. They are often followed by other fish

Left Butterfly fish (RD)

Below Spotfin lionfish (RD)

such as wrasses (Labridae) who pick up any titbits that are exposed in the process. Wrasse are among the most interesting fish: in some species an individual may grow up as a female and lay eggs, then change sex as it grows larger and become a male. Several colourful species of butterflyfish (Chaetodontidae) and angelfish (Pomacanthidae) inhabit the reef, though their numbers have been greatly reduced by over-collection for the ornamental fish trade. Smaller fish must beware of the coral grouper (*Cephalapholis miniata*), a large, orange-red carnivore that will quickly snap them up.

Many PADI-licensed dive operators run diving stations in Sri Lanka, especially on the western half of the island, from Negombo (north of Colombo) down along the coast to the south through Bentota, Beruwela, Hikkaduwa, Unawatuna and Gale. At the right time of year, when water visibility is good, a dive can be very rewarding, with many species of fish and other marine animals to be seen.

MARINE MAMMALS

From ancient times marine mammals have been a source of folklore and fable. Once they were hunted for food, blubber and other products. More recently, whale watching has become a popular ecotourism attraction worldwide. In Sri Lanka this industry is still in its infancy, held back by the availability of appropriate boats and a dearth of knowledge on the movements of cetaceans. But there is great potential.

Whales, porpoises and dolphins belong to the order Cetacea, which is represented by two living suborders: baleen whales (mysticeti) and toothed whales (odontoceti). Baleen whales have a sieve-like structure called baleen in their mouth, and two external blowholes (though the two columns of exhaled water vapor may merge into one). Toothed whales have teeth (of course!), and only one external blowhole – though internally they have two nasal passages. Five species of baleen whale and 21 species of toothed whale have been recorded in Sri Lankan waters.

BALEEN WHALES

Baleen is made of a horny substance similar to human fingernails, and is embedded in rows of plates in the gums of baleen whales. The inside of these plates is rough and bristle-like – the fineness of the bristles vary from one species to another, depending on diet. Baleen whales feed by taking in water through their mouth and expelling it through the baleen plates to sieve out the food, such as plankton or small fish. Some species use their tongue to suck in and then expel water.

Only one family of baleen whales, the Balenopteridae (rorqual whales), occurs in the waters around Sri Lanka. But this includes the blue whale (*Baleaenoptera musculus*), which is the largest animal that has ever lived, weighing up to 160 tonnes and reaching 30m in length. The good news for whale watchers is that this giant is frequently seen off Sri Lanka. Scientists suspect that there may be an annual movement of blue whales from the Arabian Sea around the south coast in about December, and back again in April, with the intervening months spent off the northeast coast – most famously off Trincomalee. The presence of blue whales here could make Sri Lanka one of the world's top whale-watching destinations, once a

Humpback whales are best identified by their long pectoral fins. (M Ushioda/WaterFrame)

permanent peace is established in the north and east. The blue whale gets its name from its mottled blue-grey colouration. It has a broad, flat, U-shaped head with a central ridge running from the blowhole to the tip of the snout. In close encounters the sheer size is awesome, with the tail flukes alone spanning six metres.

Four other species of baleen whale have been recorded in Sri Lankan waters. Of these, Bryde's whales (*Balaenoptera edeni*) are seen most often. Generally under 14m in length, this species is relatively small. Minke whales (*Balaeneoptera acutorostrata*) are smaller still, adults seldom exceeding 10m, and the few records from Sri Lanka suggest they may be more prevalent off the north-west of the island. Fin whales (*Balaenoptera physalus*), the second-largest species, and humpback whales (*Megaptera novaeangliae*) are also both occasionally seen.

TOOTHED WHALES

Toothed whales are divided into six families, of which four are represented in Sri Lankan waters. In toothed whales, the size and visibility of the teeth vary according to prey. Those that feed primarily on squid may have no visible teeth, while those that hunt fish have long jaws and protruding teeth.

The sperm whale (*Physeter macrocephalus*) is by far the world's largest toothed whale, reaching 18m in length, and is frequently recorded in waters off Trincomalee. There is speculation that a sheltered deep-water canyon here may provide a breeding ground. The waters off Trincomalee also receive a heavy discharge of nutrients from the Mahaveli River. The sperm whale is easily identified by its long, square head, whose bulbous upper section has a cavity that contains spermaceti oil – the product for which sperm whales were so ruthlessly targeted by whalers. The lower jaw is conspicuously small and thin. Females, reaching 12m, are distinctly smaller than the males.

Long-snouted spinner dolphins (*Stenella longirostris*) are probably the most abundant of Sri Lanka's marine mammals, and are often seen from the beaches of Negombo (North of Colombo) and Kirinda in the south. They reach about 2m in length, with a long snout and a dark stripe from the eye to the flippers. This species occurs in many different forms around the world.

Other dolphins regularly seen include the striped dolphin (*Stenella coeruleoalba*),

Spinner dolphin (M Ushioda/WaterFrame)

pantropical spotted dolphin (*Stenella attenuata*) and bottlenose dolphin (*Tursiops truncatus*). The striped dolphin grows to 2.7m and has a prominent stripe from the eye to the anal area, separating a bluish-grey cape from white underparts. The pantropical spotted dolphin is slightly smaller, with white underparts and a dark cape flecked with white.

Less common species in Sri Lankan waters include the Risso's dolphin (*Grampus griseus*) and Fraser's dolphin (*Lagenodelphis hosei*), both known mainly in 'bycatch' from fishing boats. The melon-headed whale (*Peponocephala electra*) is dark, with a tall dorsal fin, a triangular head and hardly any visible 'beak'. This species may be seen off the coast from Beruwela to Negombo. The false killer whale (*Pseudorca crassidens*) looks superficially similar, but is twice as large, with a distinct notch in its tail flukes. The short-finned pilot whale (*Globicephala macrorhynchus*) is usually sighted off the east coast, although there are also records from the west. The killer whale or orca (*Orcinus orca*) needs little description, its bold black-and-white markings being familiar to many people from oceanariums and the movies. This species, up to 9m in length, lives in tight-knit social groups. Some reside in one area and feed mainly on fish. Others travel widely and hunt marine mammals.

WHALE LIFE

Cetaceans are well adapted to their aquatic existence. A number of features help streamline their bodies for easier underwater locomotion: limbs modified into flippers; genitalia and teats concealed in slits; and no hair or external ears. Being mammals, of course, they must surface for air, but the location of blowholes on top of the elongated snout means that their breathing does not interfere with their forward movement. They can dive to great depths, over 2km in the case of sperm whales, and can hold their breath for long periods. Cetaceans also have the

Bottlenose dolphins are social animals, which form offshore schools of around 25 animals.
(M Bergbauer/WaterFrame)

remarkable ability to communicate over vast distances under water using low-frequency sounds – across thousand of kilometres, in the case of humpback whales and blue whales. Many species also use click-like vocalisations to echolocate – just like bats do.

Cetaceans are intelligent mammals, and have a strong social order, with family groups often staying together for generations. They generally occur in small groups, sometimes known as pods, though some species may occasionally form much larger gatherings. Many undertake yearly migrations, heading to the poles for summer and the tropical seas for winter, according to changes in water temperature and availability of food.

There are a number of theories to explain the strandings of cetaceans, one being that pressure waves generated by underwater tectonic events may damage their echolocation abilities, thus disorientating them. Some scientists believe that low-frequency sonar used by military submarines may contribute to this, and conservationists are lobbying against the use of this technology. Other threats to cetaceans include hunting, pollution and accidental trapping in fishing nets. Perhaps the most insidious lies in the contamination

Spinner dolphin (M Ushioda/WaterFrame)

of the food-web: plankton can carry traces of heavy metals and other toxic substances that accumulate in the tissue of the larger mammals that prey on them.

INDIAN DUGONG *Dugong dugong*

The dugong is unrelated to cetaceans and belongs to a separate order of marine mammals, called the Sirenia. This slow-moving, hebivorous sea mammal is widespread around the world, from Madagascar to Australia, and some scientists belive that three distinct species may occur. A few centuries ago the Indian dugong was reportedly found in groups of a few hundred. It is not clear whether these records were accurate, or a case of dolphins being mistaken for dugongs. Today, however, the dugong is very rare in Sri Lanka, with records restricted to the Gulf of Mannar. It is hunted for its flesh, despite being a protected species, and its Sinhalese name, *Muhudu oora*, means sea pig. Dugongs are found mostly in shallow sediment-rich waters around mangroves and estuaries, where they feed on sea grass.

The dugong is thought by some to have been the original source of the mermaid myth. (M Kirschner/WaterFrame)

GETTING ABOUT

A close encounter (Devaka Seneviane/Studio Times)

Scuba diving is the best way to observe hawksbill turtles. (R Dirscherl/WaterFrame)

INDEPENDENT TRAVEL

Sri Lanka is a relatively easy destination for independent travellers. There is a good network of roads and English is widely spoken. Therefore, whether you wish to hire a car at the airport or are looking to use public transport as a backpacker, it is not too difficult to get about. Wildlife is always within relatively easy reach. Even when staying at a budget beach hotel, you can easily find a *tuk tuk* (auto rickshaw) to take you on a nature excursion. Many popular tourist destinations will hire out a car for a day or more if you wish to make longer excursions. The more popular places also have a broad range of accommodation, from rooms for backpackers to small guesthouses, luxury villas and hotels. Bradt Travel Guides provide plenty of information for independent travellers.

It is possible to book an excursion to the popular national parks from nearby towns. For instance, Tissmaharama is the base for Yala and Bundala national parks, Habarana and Sigiriya for Minneriya National Park, and Nuwara Eliya for Horton Plains National Park. Both licensed and unlicensed operators will offer excursions that include a car and driver, and entry fees. Note that it is unlikely you will receive quality naturalist interpretation on these tours. Ask around for recommendations if you are travelling independently. Booking bungalows or camping inside national parks involves a lot of logistics and formalities, and even tour operators often refuse to get involved. Sri Lanka is not like Malaysia, where you can turn up at a park and pay for a campsite 'pitch' on the spot.

Entry permits to national parks and archaeological sites operate on two tiers: one for locals and the other for foreigners. The cheaper rate for locals is common in developing countries and aims to make the sites affordable to the local population. It is assumed that a foreigner on holiday is more affluent. Whilst this thinking is generally acceptable and not uncommon, the two-tier structure in Sri Lanka generates controversy, since visitor facilities for foreigners do not always justify the higher rate demanded of them.

TOURS

Despite Sri Lanka being a relatively easy destination for independent travellers, those with specialist interests or limited time may find an organised tour a better option. Birders and photographers, especially, may find that the services of a skilled guide make all the diference. Trip reports on the internet can be a good way to evaluate whether your best option is to go it alone or take a tour.

Sri Lanka has a good structure of licensed tour operators who handle ground arrangements. This could be for travellers making direct bookings, as well as travellers booking through a tour operator in their home country. Only inbound tour operators licensed by the Sri Lanka Tourist Board are supposed to handle the ground arrangements for tours. If you are making a booking from overseas, it is advisable to have your tour organised by one of the reputable companies in Sri Lanka. This will ensure a safety net of being licensed and insured. Such companies will also use reliable vehicles and dependable accommodation, plus other services.

There is a good system of licensed chauffeur guides and national guides. The latter are licensed to handle large groups. They are not allowed to take bookings directly but will be engaged by the tour operators to lead a group of clients. Some are freelance while others are exclusive to a particular company.

Serious wildlife enthusiasts, birders and photographers may be better off booking with a specialist tour operator that caters to them. The quality of the guide makes a big impact on the experience. Some specialist tour operators have chauffeur guides and national guides who are also naturalists. The national guides tend to handle the larger groups. The fee structure depends mainly on the skill level. However, national guides cost more, as they enjoy a standard of accommodation that matches that of their clients.

The cost of a tailored leopard safari or an expert-led birdwatching tour will start at about US$250 per person per day, from a specialist company. A good guide alone will cost around US$50 a day. Cheaper packages are available, but, as with so much in life, you get what you pay for.

Sri Lanka offers outstanding opportunities for elephant viewing. (GSW)

SUGGESTED ITINERARY

There are many ways in which to enjoy Sri Lanka's wildlife. Your choice of where to go will depend on your area of interest, your budget and how much time you have to spare. The following itinerary offers a broad spectrum of the island's wildlife, taking in most major habitats and principal wildlife attractions. Sri Lanka's modest size means that travelling times are relatively short, so two weeks is ample time in which to do justice to the island. There are, of course, many possible itineraries. Birdwatchers, for instance, might have different priorities. Use the information in this book to plan one that best suits your interests.

DAY 1: Arrive in Sri Lanka and transfer to Colombo for one night. Take an evening walk to Talangama to look for the western race of the purple-faced leaf monkey, also birds and nocturnal mammals such as fishing cat and yellow-striped mouse-deer.

DAY 2: After breakfast leave for Wasgomuwa for two nights. In the evening take a relaxing nature walk past the paddy fields to observe dragonflies and wetland birds.

DAY 3: Morning and afternoon game drives to Wasgomuwa National Park. Some 23 species of mammals have been recorded, including the elephant.

DAY 4: Morning game drive to Wasgomuwa National Park, before leaving for Sigiriya for two nights.

DAY 5: Visit Polonnaruwa (A UNESCO World Heritage Site), the medieval capital of Sri Lanka, for its famous troops of toque macaques (as featured in both the BBC's *Temple Troop* and *Life of Mammals*). Observe the power play between the macaques and hanuman langurs. During the afternoon, visit Minneriya National Park for elephants. In September or October, you can see more than 300 elephants gathering on the receding shores of the Minneriya Tank. At dusk look for grey loris.

DAY 6: Climb Sigiriya at dawn and look for primates. After breakfast leave for Kandy for two nights. En route, visit Dambulla Cave Temple, which is famous for its rock paintings and rock temples and is an important site for Buddhist pilgrims. The wet zone race of the toque monkey is seen easily in Kandy.

DAY 7: Morning excursion to Knuckles Wilderness Area, which is one of the most rugged and picturesque terrains in Sri Lanka. Several endemic animals are confined to the Knuckles, including the leaf-nosed lizard.

DAY 8: After breakfast leave for Nuwara Eliya for two nights. En route, visit the Temple of the Sacred Tooth Relic at Kandy, which is one the most important sacred sites in the country. From Nuwara Eliya, in the afternoon, visit Hakgala Botanical Gardens. Here you can look for the highland races of purple-faced leaf monkey and toque monkey. The toques brim with self-confidence and may approach the visitors.

DAY 9: In the morning, visit Horton Plains National Park to see cloudforest and rare montane fauna, including the endemic rhino-horned lizard. Mammal highlights include bear monkey, giant squirrel and sambar. Walk through the grasslands and cloudforest to a popular viewpoint known as World's End overlooking an 870m escarpment.

DAY 10: After breakfast leave for Yala National Park for three nights. Stay close to Yala, where the BBC's famous wildlife documentary *Leopard Hunters* was filmed. In the afternoon relax at the hotel or venture out to beachcomb.

DAY 11: Morning and evening game drives in Yala, looking out for leopards. Other large animals may include elephant, sloth bear, mugger crocodile, spotted deer, sambar, muntjac, wild pigs, wild buffalo, jackal, grey langur and mongoose.

DAY 12: Morning and evening game drives in Yala with the focus on leopards.

DAY 13: After breakfast leave for Embilipitiya. Afternoon game drive in Udawalawe National Park, where elephants are virtually guaranteed.

DAY 14: Morning, visit Uda Walawe National Park once more and leave for Negombo.

DAY 15: Departure.

A young leopard investigates a pangolin. (GSW)

129

PHOTOGRAPHY TIPS

The light is best for photography early in the morning and late in the evening. At midday, the harsh tropical sun overhead creates strong shadows – leading to subjects either lost in shade, or the sky and background bleached out. As the sun rises quickly in the tropics, the window of opportunity for photographers may be less than four hours in the whole day. A thin veil of cloud can produce diffused light that is bright, but not too harsh and produces good conditions for photography – especially for close-up subjects like flowers.

Be prepared. Take more film (if using a film camera) and batteries than you think you will need and, if shooting on digital, make sure you have spare memory cards. I once had to leave a set of leopard cubs and head back to recharge batteries when one back-up battery failed. Almost everywhere in Sri Lanka where a photographer is likely to stay will have a power supply for charging equipment. Play safe and give your equipment a full charge every evening.

Camera shake is a common problem, creating blurred or soft images. If you are handholding, the shutter speed should be faster than the reciprocal of your focal

Patient observation allows you to capture striking images, such as this hanuman langur aggression display. (GSW)

length for the images to be reasonably sharp: for example, 1/125th of a second for a 100mm lens and 1/500th for a 500mm lens. Support your camera and lens on a tripod, whenever possible, or on the edge of a vehicle's window or other surface. A small beanbag can be useful for support when in a vehicle, with a packet of rice making a handy substitute.

For landscape images, use a high f-number to maximise your depth of field. This stops down the aperture, reducing the amount of light entering the lens. Slow shutter speeds result, so a tripod is essential in some situations. For capturing action, or minimizing camera shake or subject movement, use the lowest f-number possible. This opens up the aperture and allows the fastest available shutter speed. It also creates a pleasing background blur that can throw your subject into sharp relief.

Understand the different modes of your camera. I almost always shoot in aperture priority mode. I keep the aperture open as wide as possible (lowest f-number) to maximise shutter speed. When I need more depth of field, I stop down. Some cameras have a depth of field preview button. With digital cameras, you can study your results on the spot then, if necessary, adjust and take another photograph immediately.

Black-backed dwarf kingfisher (GSW)

If you are serious about your wildlife photography, try to develop your fieldcraft. A wildlife photographer is the merger of two skilled people: a photographer and a naturalist. A naturalist's skills will help you to see more, and thus take better photographs. A good naturalist is constantly alert to possibilities – for instance, to the approach of a predator by the alarm calls of birds or other mammals. A naturalist will also know at what times of the year different species are more active or are most likely to be seen. For example, it is best to search for sloth bears in July when the palu fruit is ripening, or for elephants in August and September when 'The Gathering' takes place. Patience is truly a virtue with photography. Long waits at waterholes in Yala have rewarded me with leopards, sloth bears and many other exciting animal encounters.

On one occasion I was in Yala and observed a motionless solitary elephant with his trunk on the ground. I realised that he was communicating with another elephant by using infrasound. I stopped to see what would happen whilst other safari vehicles drove on. Soon another bull elephant came crashing in and a mighty battle kicked off. Different types of animals need different approaches. For instance, placing perches beside a pond is a good way to photograph dragonflies or kingfishers from a hide, while primates are best photographed from a popular cultural site where they have become accustomed to visitors. What you know is what you see.

FURTHER INFORMATION

BOOKS
BIRDS

Gehan's Photo Booklet: Birds of Sri Lanka and Southern India
de Silva Wijeyeratne, Eco Holidays, Colombo, 2006. Covers 263 of Sri Lanka's 444 recorded species; 42 colour plates with captioned photographs.

Shorebirds: An Artist in the Field
de Silva Wijeyeratne and Perera, Eco Holidays, Colombo, 2004. The first true 'wildlife art' book published in Sri Lanka, this showcases the work of Lester Perera, arguably Sri Lanka's best-known wildlife artist.

A Pictorial Guide and Checklist of the Birds of Sri Lanka
de Silva Wijeyeratne, Eco Holidays, Colombo, due 2007. An illustrated checklist with photographs of more than 200 species, plus a map of key birding sites, a booklist, and a discussion of nomenclature, taxonomy and status.

A Photographic Guide to the Birds of Sri Lanka
de Silva Wijeyeratne, Warakagoda and de Zylva, New Holland, London, 2000. Descriptions and photographs of 252 species, covering some of the endemics and those likely to be seen on a short visit. An accessible guide, suitable for all levels.

A Field Guide to the Birds of Sri Lanka
Harrison, Oxford University Press, Oxford, 1999. A comprehensive field guide with plates and text covering virtually every species and race recorded. Lightweight and portable; no serious birdwatcher should be without it.

A Field Guide to the Birds of Sri Lanka
Kotagama and Fernando, Wildlife Heritage Trust, Colombo, 1994. Aimed at encouraging an interest in birds amongst the wider Sri Lankan public, with 238 species illustrated in colour and a brief text.

A Birdwatcher's Guide to Sri Lanka
de Silva Wijeyeratne, Oriental Bird Club (www.orientalbirdclub.org), 1997. Remains the most detailed site guide to Sri Lanka. Copies can be ordered from the OBC web site.

INVERTEBRATES

A Selection of the Butterflies of Sri Lanka
Banks and Banks, Lake House Investments, Colombo, 1985. Butterflies are arranged by colour and size. A very useful guide for beginners.

Gehan's Photo Booklet: Dragonflies of Sri Lanka and Southern India
Bedjanic, de Silva Wijeyeratne and Conniff, Eco Holidays, Colombo, 2006. Covers 78 of Sri Lanka's 117 described species of dragonfly and damselfly; colour plates with captions.

The Butterflies of Ceylon
d'Abrera, Wildlife Heritage Trust, Colombo, 1998. Fairly comprehensive, with
good colour plates of specimens. For serious enthusiasts. Out of print in Sri Lanka,
but the UK edition can be ordered online.

The Dragonflies of Sri Lanka
de Fonseka, Wildlife Heritage Trust, Colombo. 2000. A compilation of the
literature on Sri Lankan dragonflies, with 20 colour plates.

Gehan's Photo Booklet: Butterflies of Sri Lanka and Southern India
de Silva Wijeyeratne, Eco Holidays, Colombo, 2006. Covers 96 of Sri Lanka's 243
described species of butterfly and skipper; colour plates with captioned photographs.

Ours to Protect: Sri Lanka's Biodiversity Heritage
Pethiyagoda, WHT Publications (Pvt) Limited, Colombo, 1998. A large-format
book, lavishly illustrated with photographs.

MAMMALS

Leopards and other wildlife of Yala
de Silva Wijeyeratne, Jetwing, Colombo, 2004. An attractive coffee-table book,
with authoritative text. Covers everything from large mammals to invertebrates,
plants and conservation. A useful introduction not only to Yala but also to the
other parks and reserves in Sri Lanka's dry lowlands.

Mammals of Sri Lanka
Miththapala, March for Conservation, Colombo, 1998.

Manual of the Mammals of Sri Lanka
Phillips, Wildlife and Nature Protection Society of Sri Lanka, Colombo, 1952;
2nd edition 1980. Remains the standard reference for Sri Lankan mammals.
Illustrated in black and white.

Whales & Dolphins of Sri Lanka
Ilangakoon, Wildlife Heritage Trust
(Private) Ltd, Colombo, 2001. The definitive
guide to the marine mammals of Sri Lanka.

REPTILES AND AMPHIBIANS

Amphibians of Peninsular India
Daniels, Universities Press India (Private)
Ltd. 268 pages plus photographic plates.
A good introduction to amphibian biology
with text on a selection of species
representing different families.

*A Photographic Guide to Snakes and
Other Reptiles of Sri Lanka*
Das and de Silva, New Holland, London,
2006. An excellent introduction.

Pheasant-tailed jacana (GSW)

SOCIETIES

The Sri Lanka Natural History Society (SLNHS)
email: slnhs@lanka.com.lk
An active, albeit small society with a core membership of enthusiasts and
professionals in nature conservation. It organises a varied programme of lectures
and slide presentations for its members, embracing all fields of natural history
including marine life, birds, environmental issues and photography. Also runs
regular day trips and excursions.

Field Ornithology Group of Sri Lanka (FOGSL)
Department of Zoology, University of Colombo, Colombo 3 tel: 5342609;
email: fogsl@slt.lk, www.fogsrilanka.org
The Sri Lankan representative of Bird Life International aims to become a
leading local organisation for bird study and bird conservation. It organises site
visits and lectures throughout the year. Publications include the 'Malkoha' newsletter.

Wildlife and Nature Protection Society (WNPS)
86 Rajamalwatta Rd, Battaramulla; tel: 2887390; email wnps@sltnet.lk
Publishes the biannual journals, *Loris* (in English) and *Warana* (in Sinhalese), with
current and back issues on sale at its office. Loris carries a wide range of articles,
ranging from comment and poetry to more scientific contributions.
The society also has a reasonably stocked library on ecology and natural history.

Lesser sand plovers in flight (GSW)

The Young Zoologists' Association of Sri Lanka (YZA)
National Zoological Gardens, Dehiwala; tel: 4204566; fax: 2714542
The bulk of YZA's membership is composed of schoolchildren and undergraduates,
the rest being graduates, professionals and nature lovers from all walks of life.

Ruk Rakaganno (Tree Society of Sri Lanka)
2nd Floor, The Professional Centre, 275/75 Prof Stanley Wijesundera Mawatha,
Colombo 7; tel: 2554438; email: rukraks@sltnet.lk
Set up to combat the destruction of Sri Lanka's forests, Ruk Raks aims to raise
awareness and appreciation of trees. Current activities include replanting and
awareness programmes in coastal areas, the maintenance of a nursery of
indigenous trees, and the management of the Popham Arboretum in Dambulla.
It also organises seminars and field trips.

FINDING OUT MORE
www.jetwingeco.com has over a thousand pages of information on Sri Lanka's
fauna and flora. Sign up for a quarterly 'Sri Lanka Wildlife' e-newsletter by
e-mailing gehan@jetwing.lk with 'Subscribe Wildlife News' in the message header.

Page numbers in *italics* refer
to illustrations; those in
bold to main entries.

agamids *see* lizards
'allo' mother 25
amphibians 94–8
ants 103
Anuradhapura 61
arthropods 99
Asian elephant *see* elephant

babbler
  brown-capped **73**
  Ceylon rufous 18, 55, **73**
  Ceylon scimitar 73
  dark-fronted 55
  yellow-billed 46, 53
barb
  cherry 113
  Cuming's 113, *113*
  black-lined *112*, 113, *113*
  black ruby *112*, 113
barbet
  brown-headed 52
  Ceylon small 53, **70**
  yellow-fronted *56*, 57, **70**
bat
  dog-faced 48
  Indian flying fox *47*, 48
  Indian short-nosed fruit 48,
    48
  leaf-nosed 48, *48*
bats 47–8
bear monkey *see* leaf monkey
bear *see* sloth bear
bees 103
Bellanwila Attidiya
  Sanctuary 42, 77
Block 1 (Yala) 16, 32
  see also Yala
books 132
Bolgoda Lake, 29, 42
bond group 25
buffalo, water 30, *30*
Bufo
  kotagami 95
  melanostictus 94
bulbul
  black-capped **72**
  yellow-eared 58, *58*, 72

Bundala National Park 59, 64
butterfly
  birdwing, common 107
  blue mormon 107
butterflies 105–7
carnivores 31
Cassia
  fistula 14
  auriculata 14
cat
  fishing *33*, 33–4, 50
  jungle 33
  rusty-spotted 33, **33**
caecelians 94
cats 33 *see also* leopard
centipedes 99, *99*
Ceratophora
  aspera 79
  erdelini 79
  karu 79
  stoddarti 78
  tennenti 79
cetaceans 119–24
  see also whales and dolphins
chameleon 81
charnockitic gneiss 8
Chrysopela
  ornata 84
  taprobanica 84
civets 17, 31, **38–9**, *39*
climate 6
cloudforest 1, 12–13
cobra, Indian 84, 86, *86*
Colubridae 83
combtail, paradise 112
Cophotis ceylanica 78
corals 115
Corbett's Gap 13
coucal, green-billed 69, *69*
crab
  fiddler 115
  ghost *114*, 115
crabs **114–15**, 117
crocodile
  estuarine 88
  marsh 88, *88–9*
crocodiles 88–90

damselflies *see* dragonflies
deer
  hog 27

muntjac 27, *29*
sambar *27*, 27–8
spotted 27, 28, *28*
deer 27–9
Department of Wildlife
  Conservation 16
Dipterocarpaceae 10
dolphins 120–4
dragonflies
  adjutant 108
  black-tipped flashwing 110
  dark forestwraith 109
  Frustohfer's junglewatcher
    110
  gossamerwings 110
  marsh dancer 109
  marsh skimmer 110
  mountain reedling 110
  oriental scarlet 110
  pied parasol 109
  pink skimmer 110
  scalloped spreadwing 110
  Sri Lanka cascader 110
  variable flutterer 109
  Wall's grappletail 110
  wandering wisp 109, *109*
dragonflies 102, **108–110**
drongo, Ceylon crested *55*, 74
dry zone 6
dugong 124, *124*

echolocation 47, 123
elephant, Asian *i*, *21*, *22*, *23*,
  24, *25*, **22–5**, 128
Ella Gap 8
endemic birds 68–74
Eugenia 13
Euonymus 13

Felis
  chaus 33
  rubiginosus 33
  viverrinus 34
fish 112
fishing cat *see* cat
flameback, crimson-backed
  70, *70*
flowerpecker, Legge's 73
flycatcher, dusky blue 72
flying snakes 84
'fog-stripping' 12

Forest Department 16
frogs
  Asanka's shrub 96
  Indian green 96
  Indian skipper 96
  long-snouted 96, *96*
  spotted tree 96
  Sri Lanka bullfrog 96
frogs 94–6
fruit bat 48

Galle 44
gathering *see* 'The Gathering'
gecko
  bark 80, *80*
  Brooke's house 80
  Common house 80, *80*
  termite-hill 80
geckos 79
geology 8
golden jackal *see* jackal
golden palm-civet *see*
  palm-civet
Gondwanaland 8, 11
grassland 15
green-pigeon, Ceylon 68

Hakgala 13, 44
hanging parrot, Ceylon 68, *68*
hanuman langur 28, **42**, *43*,
  128, *130*
hare, black-naped 49, *49*, 50
Hemidactylus
  brooki 80
  frenatus 80
  leschenaultii 80
  triedrus 80
Herpestes
  edwardsi 39
  fuscus 39
  smithii 39
  vitticollis 39
Herpestidae 38
hill-myna, Ceylon 74
hill zone 6
hornbill, Ceylon grey 70, *71*
Horton Plains National Park
  7, 8, *9*, 13, **19**, *19*, 25, 26, 27,
  40

Ilex 13

invertebrates 97–110

Jacobson's organ 82
jackal 17, **34–35** *34*, *35*
jungle cat 33
junglefowl, Ceylon 68, *68*

Kandy 32, 39, 44, 128
Kanneliya-Nakiyadeniya-
  Dediyagala 11, 44
Kashmir flycatcher 59
Kaudulla National Park **18**, 22
Knuckles 13, 40
Kotte 34
krait
  common 86
  Sri Lankan 86

Laughingthrush, ashy-
  headed 73
leeches 98
leopard 16, **31–2**, *31*, *32*, 127,
  129
Lepidoptera 102, 105–7
lizard
  black-dewlap 78
  black-lipped *i*, 13, *13*
  crestless 79
  dwarf 19, **78**
  Erdelen's 79
  hump-nosed 79
  kangaroo 78
  Karu's 79
  leaf-nosed 79
  maculate 79
  painted-lip 79
  rhino-horned 78, *78*
  rough-nosed 79
  whistling 79, *79*
lizards 76–81
loris
  red 40
  grey 40, *40*, 128
lowlands 6
LTTE (Liberation Tigers of
  Tamil Eelam) 2, 19

Mabuya
  carinata 80
  macularia 80
Macaca sinica 40

magpie, Ceylon blue 74, *74*
maila 14
malkoha, red-faced *57*, 69
mammals 21
mangroves 15, *15*
Mannar 66
mee tree 14, 37
melanistic 31
Mesozoic 8
Microhylidae 94
millipedes 99
Miocene 8
Minneriya National Park 2, **18**
molluscs 115, 117
mongoose
  brown 39, 50
  grey 39
  ruddy *38*, 39
  stripe-necked *38*, 39
mongooses 38–9
monitor
  land *75*, 76
  water 76, *76*
monitors 76–7
monsoons **6**, 7
monkey
  leaf 40–2, *41*, *42*, *44*, 128–9
  toque monkey *3*, 42, *43*, 128
mouse-deer
  white-spotted 29
  yellow-striped 29, 50
mouse-deer 29
musth 25
Muthurajawela 35

Nephila spp. 100
nightjar
  Indian 60
  Jerdon's 60
nocturnal wildlife 50
Nuwara Eliya 58, 78

octopus 117
Odonata 102, **108–110**
otter 39
owl
  brown fish 50, *50*
  Serendib scops *51*, 69
Owlet, chestnut-backed 69

paccinian corpuscles 23

Palatupana Salt Pans 59
palm-civet
  common 39
  golden 39
palu 14, 16, 37
panthera pardus 31
pangolin 49, *49*, *129*
parakeet, Layard's 69
Peak Wilderness Sanctuary 13
peneplains 8
Petaurista petaurista 45
Petinomys fuscocapillus 45
photography 130
Precambrian 8
Prunus 13
pig, wild 26, *26*
Polonnaruwa 2, 40
porcupine 49
Presbytis
  entellus 40
  senex 40
primates 40–41
python, Indian *82*, 83

rainforest **10–11**, 55–7
ranawara 14
Ranidae 94
rat
  antelope 49
  Indian bandicoot 49
Rhododendron 13
Ruhunu *see* Yala

scorpions 100
sea anemones 115, *115*
seabirds 66
shrew
  common musk 49
  pygmy 49
shrews 49
Sigiriya **20**, 40, 128
Sinharaja Rainforest *10*, **18**, *18*, 107, 110
skinks 81
sloth bear *36*, *37*, 37–8
snails 98
snake bites 87
snakes 82–7
snorkelling 7
spiders 100–102

spurfowl, Ceylon 68
squirrel
  dusky 46
  flame-striped 46
  giant *45*, 47
  palm 46, *46*
squirrels 45–7
star fish 117, *117*
starling, white-faced 74
Strobilanthes 13
Suidae 26
Suncus
  etruscus 49
  murinus 49
Syzigium 13
swallow, Ceylon 70

Talangama Wetland **20**, 29, 44, 50, 77, 128
Tamil Tigers *see* LTTE
taxonomic order 3
termites 37, **104**, *104*
terrapins 91
'The Gathering' 15, 19, 22, 131
thorn forest 15
thrush
  Ceylon scaly 72
  spot-winged 72, *72*
toque macaque
  see also toque monkey
tortoise, star 91, *91*
tours 127
Trincomalee 120
tsunami 2, 3
turtle
  flapshell 91
  green *90*, 93
  hawksbill 93, *126*
  leatherback 93, *93*
  loggerhead *92*, 93, *93*
  olive ridley 93
  spotted black 91
turtles 91–3

Uda Walawe National Park **17**, *17*, 22, 33, 60, 129
Udawattakale 44
underwater 111–24
ungulates 26

Vaccinium 13
Vatica 11 *see also* Dipterocarpaceae
Vedda people 38
Vijayan 8
villus 19 *see also* Wilpattu National Park
viper
  hump-nosed 85
  Russell's 85, *87*
  saw-scaled 85

waders 65
warbler, Ceylon bush 73
Wasgomuwa National Park *14*, **17**, 128
wasps 103
water buffalo *see* buffalo
water monitor *see* monitors
waxtail
  painted 109
  yellow 109
weather 6
weera 14
wet zone 6
wetlands 62–3 *see also* Bundala and Talangama
whale
  blue 119
  Bryde's 120
  minke 120
  humpback 120, *120*
  fin 120
  sperm 120
whales 119–124
when to travel 7
whistling-thrush 13, *13*, 19, 58, 72, **72**
white-eye, Ceylon 74, *74*
Wilpattu National Park **19**, 27
woodapple tree 14
wood-shrike, Ceylon 70, **72**
wood spider 100, *101*

Yala (Ruhunu) National Park **16**, 23, 37, 60

zone, dry 6
  wet 6

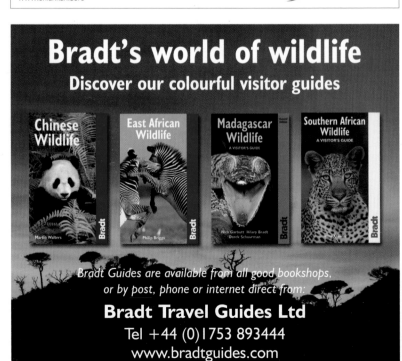